The Empowered Investor

The Empowered Investor

A Canadian Guide to Building a
Better Investment Experience

NEW AND REVISED THIRD EDITION

Keith Matthews

For copies of this book or permission to reproduce,
please contact the author:
Keith Matthews
Partner & Portfolio Manager
Tulett, Matthews & Associates Inc.
3535 St-Charles Blvd, Suite 703
Kirkland, Quebec
514-695-0096 (106)
keith@tma-invest.com

Published by
Tulett, Matthews & Associates Inc.
Kirkland, Quebec
www.tma-invest.com

Printed in Canada

LIBRARY AND ARCHIVES CANADA CATALOGUING IN
PUBLICATION

Matthews, Keith, 1963–
The empowered investor: a canadian guide to building a
better investment experience / Keith Matthews. – 3rd ed.

Includes bibliographical references
ISBN 978-0-9919783-0-4
ISBN (Ebook): 978-0-9919783-1-1

1. Investments   2. Portfolio management   I. Title

HG4527.M37   2013   332.6   C2013-907281-X

Set in 11/15 Minion Pro with Futura
Book design & typesetting by Garet Markvoort, zijn digital

IMPORTANT NOTE

This book contains the opinions of the author but not necessarily those of Tulett, Matthews & Associates Inc., and does not represent a recommendation of any particular security, strategy, or investment product. The opinions of the author are subject to change without notice.

All efforts have been made to assure the accuracy and integrity of the information presented in this book. Although all facts have been obtained from sources believed to be reliable, the information is not guaranteed, and neither the author nor the publisher is liable for any errors, omissions, or contradictions found in the text.

Investments and investing strategies should be evaluated based on your own objectives. Readers should use their best judgment and consult a financial expert prior to making any investment decisions based on the information found in this book.

To my wonderful wife Caroline,
the most courageous person I know

CONTENTS

CONTENTS

Introduction

As I sit down to write the third edition of *The Empowered Investor*, I find myself looking back on my career as a financial advisor and the circumstances that have brought me to where I am today. It might surprise some of you to know that, growing up, I never aspired to a career in finance. My dream was to follow in my father's footsteps and become an engineer. As a child I travelled the world accompanying him on his projects—from Montreal to Sri Lanka to Singapore—but my dreams took a backseat to reality as I prepared to graduate from high school. Although life was good for my family, like many other Canadians we were tested by the 1981 recession. My father's engineering jobs dried up and suddenly I realized that becoming an engineer was not protection enough against the turbulence of the economy. I had been an avid sailor my entire life and I sought a career that could steer me through whatever storms lay ahead. Following the completion of my CEGEP science degree, I decided to give up engineering to pursue a career in business.

I enrolled at Concordia University in 1984. My most significant lessons came not at the hands of my professors, but from the pages of *Fortune Magazine*. For two years on the bus to and from school, I read *Fortune* cover to cover. I was entranced by the stories of young Wall Street hotshots who were the key players behind multi-million-dollar merger and acquisition deals. I was determined to become a Wall Street investment banker like them.

I resolved to do whatever it took to become like the men I read about in *Fortune*, many of whom were just a few years older than myself. I knew that to even be looked at by one of the major Wall Street firms, I would need to graduate at the top of my class with an MBA from a prestigious school. And to be accepted into such an MBA program, I would need to graduate at the top of my undergraduate class. I was committed to success.

In 1987 I graduated with a Bachelor of Commerce degree from Concordia University and applied and was accepted to the University of Western Ontario, the only school in Canada at the time whose MBA program successfully prepared its students to work on Wall Street. My admission came with one key condition: that I work for two years and earn experience in the real world. In order to sail into business school with the laurels of my success firmly in place, I felt I needed to make it in the Big Smoke—Toronto.

To that end, I sent my resumé to all the brokerage firms, banks, and trust companies in Toronto, confident that the offers would come my way. After all, I had been a very good student, was a hard worker, and had always landed on my feet. The stock market crash of October 1987 occurred a mere week after my arrival in Toronto—and served to check the hubris of youth! Every door on Bay Street swiftly closed to new applicants and every company to which I had sent my resumé immediately instituted a hiring freeze. My first experience with the real-life world of finance was very different from what I had imagined. I had spent three years studying portfolio theory, diversification concepts, and other finance-related topics; now I watched TV reports and read newspaper articles that highlighted personal investing stories charged with emotion, hype, and sheer panic. These experiences seemed completely removed from what I had studied in the classroom.

As we know, the markets recovered and moved on. After working in a factory and as a mail courier, I landed a good position as an account manager in commercial lending with TD Bank. While I loved my stay in Toronto and look back on those years with much fondness, I had learned an important lesson—one that was to prove far more valuable than anything I learned at the bank. As a finance grad embarking on a career, I witnessed bold optimism and extreme pessimism, all within a twelve-month period. The mood of investors and the investment industry itself followed the gyrations of the market—and had affected me personally. Without warning, my career opportunities were in a shambles; just as suddenly—with a flip of the coin and a rising economy—they were very promising. I gave up engineering because I wanted a career that would give me stability in unstable times, yet the course I was on seemed no less treacherous than any other profession. I began to seek out sound financial strategies that would prosper no matter which way the winds of the market blew. This experience became the seed of an idea that would come to full bloom nearly twenty years later with the first edition of *The Empowered Investor.*

In 1989, I began the first year of my MBA at Western, knowing what would be required of me to make it to the next level. With my dreams never far from my mind, I set out to be the best in my class. At the end of my first year, I was on the honour roll and I knew that it would only be a matter of time before the big Wall Street firms took notice.

But then something strange began to happen: the more time I spent working with people in finance, the more I realized that I wasn't cut out for it. It wasn't that I lacked the skills or the determination; I just didn't have the greed that seemed to be a prerequisite for succeeding on Wall Street. Although I wanted to make money and be as successful as the men I read about in *Fortune*, I wasn't willing to betray my honesty and integrity.

As someone who was so focused on navigating his way through the stormiest seas, this realization left me rudderless. I had everything I needed to do the job I had always wanted except the desire to do it. I was shaken to the core.

Returning to Montreal in search of a new career path, I found that, once again, every door was closed. Canada had entered a recession in 1991 and very high unemployment followed for many years. Job prospects were bleak, with unemployment peaking at 11.4% (to put this into perspective, the current unemployment rate of the European Union is 11.8%). I took jobs wherever I could find them but friends eventually suggested that I return to finance. Although I was wary, I needed work and I already had the necessary training. I applied for an open position at Casgrain and Company, a Montreal bond-trading firm, and after a rigorous interview process I was hired.

I went to work on my first day and sat down at my desk. I stared at the numbers ticking by on three computer screens and asked myself what I was thinking. I had already made up my mind that the finance business wasn't for me, yet here I was at the trading desk with a single goal—make money.

Knowing that my chances of finding another job in that economy were slim, I buckled down and committed myself to doing the best I could. Looking back now, I realize that my years studying at Concordia and Western were only introductory courses to the thorough education I received at Casgrain. The investment lessons to which I was exposed are the foundation of the philosophy I use today.

After working at Casgrain for four years, I experienced two 'aha' moments that would forever shape my knowledge of investments. The first occurred on the bond desk when a news wire service announced that a major global brokerage firm had suddenly reduced its recommended equity allocations to Canadian equity for their institutional clients. Word spread like wildfire through the Canadian investment community. In and of itself, a recommendation such as this was not unusual: the odd part was what happened next. Just a few months later, although nothing significant had changed in Canada's economic outlook, the same brokerage firm reversed its initial recommendation and advised clients to increase the allocation to Canadian equities. The reversal made little sense to me, but the seasoned traders said it happened all the time. I began to wonder if market forecasting and brokerage firm recommendations were more of a game than a science.

The second moment came when I looked up the performance rankings of the bond managers we called on and serviced. Most traders do not care about the performance of the pension managers—they simply want lots of trade volume. But I wanted to get a better understanding of one particular manager; a brash and arrogant man who was ultra-confident in his calls. To my complete shock, the report concluded that he had fourth-quartile performance, which essentially meant he was not doing his job well relative to other comparable managers. I couldn't believe it. How could someone with such poor performance have such a strong presence in the industry? Through my later observations and research, I learned that this is not unusual but rather part and parcel of the investment business.

Although my primary job at Casgrain was to trade as many bonds as possible, I began to develop a passion for studying the best strategies to become a successful long-term investor. The more people asked me for investment advice, the more I realized that there were very few advisors catering to their investors' long-term goals. I saw an opportunity to take what I had studied and what I had done in the world of institutional investing and combine that with my belief that the best way to help clients was to provide value-added advice that enabled them to reach their goals. My idea was simple: build a portfolio service that provided straight-forward, conflict-free advice and clarity to private clients.

In 1997, despite the pressure of raising a young family, I left the lucrative world of bond trading—with the support of my wife, Caroline—for the uncertainty of fee-based, private client management. I had no clients, but I had a consultative approach to client service that embraced a philosophy of allocating assets on the basis of a limited selection of index-based building blocks.

Since 1997, I have focused on building the best possible investment service for private clients. Thanks to technology and accessible global partnerships, Tulett, Matthews & Associates, Inc. has been able to execute investment strategies that were once reserved only for the largest pension funds in the country.

The Empowered Investor is the culmination of more than twenty years of trying to better understand where investment returns come from, what obstacles keep investors from succeeding, what investment vehicles work best, and how to bring it all together so that investors can increase the odds of creating a successful investment experience for themselves and their families. The success of the first two editions exceeded my expectations and reflected the very real need for concrete answers to these questions. This book is a living guide to timeless investing principles that apply just as well in bull markets as they do in bear markets. Given the recent gyrations of the market and the circumstances surrounding the 2008–09 credit crisis, I believe that the lessons in this book are as valuable now as they ever were.

This guide continues to answer the need of Canadian investors for a practical tool that highlights, step by step, the key principles required to achieve investing success. *The Empowered Investor* makes readers aware that these principles, strategies, and concepts exist—and that they work. Since the success of any educational guide is rooted in its ability to communicate complex ideas simply, this book aims to bring clarity and vision to individual investors in a down-to-earth style.

Dispensing with hype, *The Empowered Investor* offers time-tested blueprints for financial success and features a selection of the best of the best in financial thinking—including Nobel Prize–winning strategies—to demonstrate the optimal solutions for investors to use in their portfolios. These investment principles are universal: they are equally as applicable to a modest RRSP account as to a hundred-million-dollar foundation plan.

In this book you will find:

- a review of the major challenges and investment pitfalls that investors face;
- leading-edge portfolio management concepts and solutions;
- a debunking of investment myths;
- research findings that every savvy investor should know;
- a thorough, straightforward, and practical section outlining eight basic principles to help you become a better investor

I hope this guide will provide invaluable insights to help you create a successful investment experience. By discovering the investment strategies that many of Canada's largest companies, major universities, and wealthy families implement with their own investments, you will gain the knowledge you need to make these strategies work for you.

The strategies in this book are supported by evidence-based research and findings. Evidence-based information is the opposite of the hype often found in today's investment literature. Evidence-based information is just that, based on evidence—data and research on what is actually happening in the real investment world. It is precise, informative, and credible.

Although many wealthy people have been investing in capital markets for over a century, most Canadian investors only began investing in these markets in the last two decades (with the real explosive growth occurring in the 1990s). The facts presented in this book are the relevant and credible recorded outcomes of the actual investment experiences of this large group of recent investors.

Another of this book's goals is to make the content relevant to many groups of readers—from the neophyte investor who is simply trying to understand more about investment concepts in general to the sophisticated, experienced investor who is well-read on many investment topics. Finding the right balance of information, communication style, and research was one of the biggest challenges in writing this guide—and caused this author many sleepless nights.

I also wanted to communicate these investment principles and concepts using language that was clear and easy to understand. I have purposely included many examples, anecdotes, and real-life comparisons to better illustrate and communicate investment concepts. The writing tone is intended to be accessible to all, to treat all readers with respect, and to bring clarification to the sometimes complex world of investment management.

To me, the title *The Empowered Investor* was the best expression of the knowledge, success, power, and peace of mind that can result from integrating the concepts in this book into your investment strategy. I cannot take credit for discovering these concepts; however, I do take pride in bringing them to you in an accessible style that I think many investors will be able to identify with and follow. Writing this guide has been an amazing experience for me. It is my sincere hope that it brings you two benefits: the satisfaction that comes from informing yourself and taking action, and the positive long-term investment results that derive from becoming an *empowered investor*.

The Empowered Investor

1

Beware the Eight Common Investment Pitfalls

BECOMING AWARE IS HALF THE BATTLE

To ensure a prosperous and financially secure future, we need to understand the potential roadblocks that can prevent us from succeeding. All too often, investors rush to implement a solution or buy an investment hoping that it will fill the gap created by previous portfolio hiccups, shortfalls, or downright mistakes. The desire to repair our immediate investment concerns may be quite valid; however, short-term adjustments usually do not result in any meaningful long-term impact. For the winning strategies discussed in *The Empowered Investor* to pay off in the long run, before putting these strategies to work investors must be aware of the pitfalls that await the unsuspecting. Knowing the rules of the playing field can save you a lot of headaches down the road—and dramatically improve your odds of future success.

While the eight common investment pitfalls discussed in this chapter are not new, they are now more relevant than ever. Investors are more likely to make knee-jerk decisions during periods of extreme volatility, which is precisely what we have endured since the financial crisis of 2008. Unfortunately, the data on investor response are not encouraging. Figure 1 is a dramatic illustration of how investors have reacted to market moves in recent years. The blue line represents global stock market returns between 2006 and 2010, while the blue bars represent the amount of money added to (or removed from) equity mutual funds during that period. The correlation is remarkable: investors reliably poured new money into equities *after* they had gone up in value

Figure 1: Emotional Investing

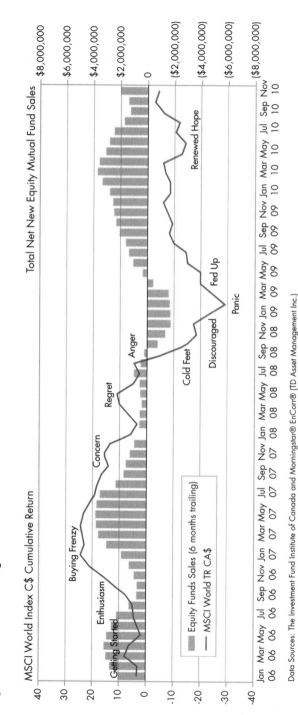

Data Sources: The Investment Fund Institute of Canada and Morningstar® EnCorr® (TD Asset Management Inc.)

Total Net New Equity Mutual Fund Sales vs. Morgan Stanley Capital International World Index (MSCI) C$, January 2006–November 2010

and pulled money out of the markets *after* prices declined. In other words, they bought high and sold low with depressing consistency.

As we will see, errors like these are often caused by our emotional attachment to money. Family finances and investing stir up our most primal feelings of security and our desire to "make it" in life. Wrestling with these feelings while riding the roller-coaster of stock and bond returns may lead us to make portfolio decisions that we later regret.

Thanks to the new field of behavioural finance, we now know that humans have biases and filters that cloud our financial judgment and ultimately lead to poor decisions about when to buy or sell assets. While some of these biases are positive attributes in other areas of life, they can be disastrous in investing. For example, high levels of confidence may help you in a job interview, but bravado as an investor can lead to self-destructive behaviour.

What is the value of reviewing these common investing pitfalls? First, simply becoming aware of them can help you avoid the costly mistakes that plague many investors. It will also provide you with a foundation on which to base your understanding of the winning investment principles discussed in *The Empowered Investor*.

More experienced investors may feel they are already aware of these common mistakes. However, I sincerely recommend reviewing these eight pitfalls annually. Constant vigilance has tremendous value when it comes to your portfolio. I can't count the number of times I have met serious and smart investors who have told me, "I did everything right for ten years and I know all about investment pitfalls; but last year I let my emotions drive me to do something foolish—and it really set me back!"

Pitfall 1: Lack of an Investment Policy Statement (IPS)

The lack of a clear vision is the root cause of the majority of challenges faced by investors. Many people feel confused or apprehensive when it comes to their portfolio—and rightfully so. They're bombarded with all kinds of information and they don't know what it means for them. Investing is a daunting task and for many people it is uncharted territory. An investment policy statement (or investment plan) acts as a map to guide you along your investment journey by taking the following into account:

- your long-term objectives
- your time horizon
- your saving and spending rates
- diversification decisions for your portfolio
- your tax consequences
- associated risks with your portfolio strategy
- rules of engagement for dealing with industry professionals

Think of these as landmarks that your IPS will help you navigate. By putting your plan in writing and linking it with your investment philosophy, you create a blueprint for your investments that will help guide you along the path to achieving your goals. A good IPS highlights how all the moving parts work together and elaborates on the decision-making process used to execute the investment philosophy for you and your family.

Why is it important to have an investment plan? We work with plans when we build our homes or cottages; successful entrepreneurs and business owners have a vision and a plan; companies and organizations have them as well; so too should our investments. The world of investing is always changing, but the approach detailed in this book proves that a well-constructed and disciplined plan will allow you to be well-positioned during good times and bad. Instead of worrying about the challenges presented in the short term, a sound investment plan will help you become better informed about the relationship between returns, risk, and time horizons. It will shift the focus to the proper management of your long-term portfolio. By prioritizing the long-term health of your investments, you'll be better positioned to weather challenges and common pitfalls in the short term. An IPS is such a key component of success that I never work without one when serving my clients.

Pitfall 2: Lack of an Investment Philosophy

An investment philosophy (also called investment strategy) is a set of guiding principles that shape and inform an individual's, an advisor's, or an advisory firm's investment decision-making process. While an IPS can be thought of as a map, your investment philosophy is a code of conduct that defines how your money will be managed. The investment philosophy is the star by which you steer; it is the approach you take when it comes to managing your money.

Your investment philosophy determines how you behave as an investor. There's an old adage that says "if you don't stand for something, you'll fall for anything." Without a clear belief system to govern how you invest, you risk falling into the other pitfalls on this list.

When I speak to investors who are frustrated or confused about their portfolio, or are having a hard time understanding the big picture, I often find that they (or their advisor) either don't have, or fail to adhere to, an investment philosophy. They claim that their approach to investing is to buy "good deals." This does not constitute an investment philosophy and such behaviour will more often than not lead to chaotic, random, and risky portfolio construction. Baseball managers don't tell their batters to swing for the fence on each pitch. Instead, they protect the plate and hit what they can in order to get on base. An investment philosophy has a set of principles and guidelines that determines which pitches you swing for and which you don't. It provides direction and perspective for the decisions you should and shouldn't make with your investments.

The Empowered Investor highlights eight key principles that, when implemented together, form a powerful and all-encompassing investment philosophy.

Pitfall 3: Being Unaware of the Mathematics of Sustainable Portfolios

Canadians remain unaware of or unable to appreciate the significance of the mathematics of sustainability, despite the fact that numbers don't lie. We're not living sustainable lifestyles. Sustainability means taking proper care of our resources so that we may continue to use them in the future. In financial terms, it means setting aside enough money for financial independence and a fiscally healthy retirement. Most of us are not doing this.

In 1989, Canadians were introduced to David Chilton's *The Wealthy Barber*, which suggests investing a percentage of what you earn in long-term growth. Be it 10%, 15%, or 20% (perhaps even 30% if you have neglected your savings), you should set aside an annual percentage of your earnings for your retirement. The amount you save affects how much you will be able to draw down after you retire. Sustainable portfolio draw-downs must be used throughout retirement. For 60-, 65-, and 70-year-olds who want to have thirty years of inflation-protected retirement funding, prudent and conservative amounts to withdraw each year are 3%, 4%, and 5%, respectively. However, many Canadians reach the age of retirement with the impression that they can draw down 10%, 15%, or even 20% of their portfolios. Once again, this is a case of people misunderstanding or simply being unaware of the mathematics of financially sustainable portfolios.

Sustainability is the key word when it comes to planning for retirement. Ask yourself, "Is the life I live now going to be sustainable in the future?" The answer should always be a resounding "yes." Today's challenge, unfortunately, is that you almost need to be an actuary in order to appreciate the consequences that arise from not living a sustainable lifestyle. At a bare minimum, Canadians need to become aware of the math involved in a sustainable lifestyle and the factors that affect its outcome. We are seeing the effects this lack of sustainability has had on Europe. Entire nations are in crisis because governments and people were unable to grasp the mathematics of sustainable economies.

By not adhering to a sustainable financial lifestyle, investors often fall into the trap of looking for solutions that will recover the ground they've lost due to their lack of necessary savings. This emotional reaction causes investors to have unreasonable expectations of their investments and costs them in the long run. Instead of staying the course laid out by their IPS (assuming they have one), the desire to remedy their

lack of savings and ensure their retirement well-being may lead investors to gamble, speculate, and chase performance.

It is impossible to overstate the importance of understanding the
mathematics of sustainability.

Pitfall 4: Trying to Profit by Timing the Market

A classic study of American investors by DALBAR—one of North
America's leading financial services research firms—clearly shows the
negative effects of trying to time the market. DALBAR tracked monthly
cash flows in and out of mutual funds from 1993 through 2012 and
came to the following dismal conclusions: over the last twenty years,
the average U.S. equity fund investor earned 4.25% annually, falling far
short of the 8.21% the S&P 500 earned over that period; the average
bond fund investor earned 0.98% annually, compared with the Barclays
Aggregate Bond Index return of 6.34%.

Table 1 shows the 1-, 3-, 5-, 10-, and 20-year annualized returns for
the average equity and fixed income investor in the U.S. When comparing these annualized returns to corresponding benchmarks, we see
both equity and fixed income mutual fund investors underperforming
the market in nearly every time frame.

Investors can capture everything the markets have to give (minus
very small fees) simply by staying invested at all times. But we are
humans with emotions and instead of sticking to time-tested, winning
strategies based on diversification and long-term asset allocation, we
often engage in market timing. We buy or sell assets based on predictions and the emotions we feel at the time. Inevitably, it ends up costing
us in the long run.

Current world events or media frenzy, rather than future economic
reality, can drive panicked investors to sell. Whether caused by 9/11,
the financial crisis of 2008, or the ongoing debt problems in Europe,
anxiety spurs investors into wild selling sprees. DALBAR's 2013 survey
revealed that investors continue to make these same mistakes. The fear
generated by negative headlines or a lacklustre earnings report prompts
investors to deviate from their plan and sell their assets. They then miss

Table 1: % Annualized Fund Investor Returns vs. Benchmark
(as of 31 December 2012)

	Avg. Equity Investor	S&P 500	Difference	Avg. Fixed Income Investor	Barclays Aggregate Bond Index	Difference
20-year	4.25	8.21	-3.96	0.98	6.34	-5.36
10-year	6.05	7.10	-1.05	1.17	5.18	-4.01
5-year	-0.84	1.66	-2.50	1.64	5.95	-4.31
3-year	7.63	10.87	-3.24	2.85	6.19	-3.34
1-year	15.56	15.98	-0.42	4.68	4.21	+0.47

Source: Quantitative Analysis of Investor Behavior 2013, DALBAR, Inc.

the recoveries that inevitably follow and buy back in only after prices have increased. Countless studies and reports have proven that you are better off staying in the market throughout the good times and the bad.

Market timing is not always about emotions: some people insist that they can use charts and other indicators to determine the best times to get in or out of the market. In an article in the *Journal of Financial Research*, Larry L. Fisher and Meir Statman analyzed various market-timing models that try to determine when the market is "expensive" and should be sold, or "inexpensive" and should be bought. Figure 2 shows that the "Stock Buy and Hold" approach would have provided the highest growth of assets compared to timing the market based on P/E trading rules.

It may seem reasonable to try to time your entry into and exit from the equity markets, but the strategy comes with huge risks. This is one of the biggest mistakes you can make, and it can easily lead to falling short of your investment objectives.

Pitfall 5: Chasing Performance

Have you ever bought a stock that looked like a superstar only to watch it fall by 30% before unloading it? I have yet to meet an investor (myself

Figure 2: Market Timing Falls Short

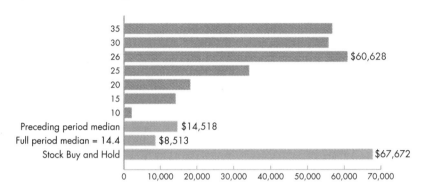

Market Timing with P/E Trading Rules: United States 1871–2002. Trading rules: Investors have $1 at the beginning of 1871 and that money accumulates over time as it is invested in stocks or T-bills. Investors switch from T-bills to stocks when the P/E ratio is lower than the P/E ratio in the trading rule and back to T-bills when it is higher. For example, the trading rule associated with a P/E ratio of 26 calls for switching from T-bills to stocks when the P/E ratio is lower than 26 and back to T-bills when the P/E ratio is higher. The study examined trading rules with P/E as integers from 5 to 40, but we report only some, including the one with the highest accumulation.

Source: Kenneth L. Fisher and Meir Statman, "Market Timing in Regressions and Reality," *Journal of Financial Research* 29, no. 3 (Fall 2006): 293–304

included) who has not admitted to buying high and selling low at least once in his or her lifetime. The equity markets are filled with buyers and sellers who act on emotion and respond to media hype. The cold, hard truth of the matter is that investors who do not separate themselves from their emotions will in the end be separated from their money.

Buying individual stocks at their highs and chasing after hot fund managers and asset class performance are not new phenomena. When we make the initial purchase, we undoubtedly feel that we have a good reason. Usually a sizzling story is behind the stock's recent appreciation. We are told that it is a "new world" and that prices can still go up. You say to yourself, "What if I miss this great buying opportunity?" or "This is the stock that will do wonders for my portfolio," and, bingo! It's done. You just bought a stock at its historic high!

Investors buying at high levels in industries such as technology, pharmaceuticals, banking, real estate, consumer retail, and commodities have all landed in hot water during the last twenty-five years or so. While these sectors should all be part of a long-term portfolio, trying to determine which one will be the next hot performer is not the ticket to untold riches.

Buying high and selling low can devastate the long-term success of your portfolio. The investment strategies in this book will help you keep your emotions at bay and show you how to build a portfolio in a structured, rigorous, and disciplined way—one that helps protect you from this common investment pitfall.

Pitfall 6: Lack of Proper Diversification

Most investors know that it is prudent to diversify, but do they truly practice diversification in their portfolios? Many people who believe they are well diversified actually have highly-concentrated and risky portfolios. The lack of proper diversification (by asset class, industrial sector, geographic region, and currency) ranks as one of the most serious investment pitfalls, and it exposes many people to potentially large losses. Many investors and some advisors don't seem to fully appreciate and understand this concept. They believe owning fifteen stocks or ten mutual funds makes them diversified. But too much overlap results in bad diversification, which can be costly in the long term. It is not the number of stocks alone that provides diversity, but the variety.

Why do investors forego the benefits of diversification? One reason is that over-confident investors believe they have the knowledge or skill to identify which sectors or asset classes will be the best performers in the near future. To these people, diversifying their portfolios would be admitting that they are too timid or too ignorant to make bold moves; instead they place large bets on a few companies or a few sectors.

For other investors, the problem is simply a lack of awareness of the difference between good and bad diversification. They might feel that they are enjoying the benefits of diversification because they have many mutual funds (or many advisors); however, if the funds or investments have overlapping exposure to certain industries, their portfolios may be highly ineffective.

While, on occasion, highly-concentrated portfolios can lead to significant gains, the lack of proper diversification exposes investors to potential losses that may be just as large—or larger. All too often, investors only consider the upside and ignore the downside.

Proper diversification also protects you from unexpected events. The term "black swan" comes from the ancient misconception that all swans were white—it was originally used as a metaphor for something that did not exist. When black swans were discovered in Australia in the seventeenth century, the term took on a new meaning: it describes something that is considered impossible until it actually comes to pass. In his book *The Black Swan*, Nassim Taleb extends the metaphor to the financial world. He explains that a black swan is a market event that is unpredictable and has a massive impact. More importantly, Taleb says, we concoct an explanation after the fact to make the event appear less random and more predictable than it actually was. In the financial world, the astonishing success of Google was a black swan; 9/11 and the collapse of Lehman Brothers in 2008 were black swans as well.

Black swan events can have profound effects on a concentrated portfolio, but their impact can be mitigated by diversifying your exposure to risk. You cannot prepare for specific black swans: by definition, they are unpredictable. However, by remaining broadly diversified, you can ensure that your portfolio will not be devastated by any single event.

Pitfall 7: Building Portfolios Based on "Expert" Predictions

It is important to understand and accept that the financial industry depends on predictions to build its value propositions. Wall Street, Bay Street, the brokerage industry, and the financial advisory business have used slick marketing campaigns to position themselves as experts at predicting the markets. These predictions usually appear in the form of stock tips, market analyses, or mutual fund reports. How useful is this "expert" information? The evidence clearly shows that the accuracy of these predictions is hit and miss. Yet, poor track records do not stop

Table 2: Stock Market Forecasting Abilities of Market Gurus

Market Pundits	Batting Average
Abby Joseph Cohen	0.128
Edward Kerschner	0.136
Jeffery Applegate	0.147
Thomas Galvin	0.147
Elaine Garzarelli	0.152
Edward Yardeni	0.152
Lazlo Birinyi	0.157
David Jones	0.164
Richard Bernstein	0.183
Bill Gross	0.189
Tobias Levkovich	0.200
Edward Hyman	0.236

Source: Smartmoney.com (survey conducted from 1997–2002)

so-called investment gurus and financial market pundits from coming up with ever more elaborate scenarios with increasing certainty. They're the white noise of the investment world and you will be much better off once you tune them out.

Just how far off the mark are these predictions? SmartMoney.com tracked the forecasts of Wall Street equity market strategists during the bull and bear markets of 1997 to 2002. As table 2 shows, these market pundits—all of whom were regularly quoted for their views on market direction—did not have good batting averages.

In hindsight, this six-year survey period offered market strategists a once-in-a-lifetime opportunity to predict market movements that included a major surge followed by a historic meltdown. Not one of them was able to predict these major events.

The accuracy of market predictions has not improved in recent years. The most telling example involves the predictions (and lack thereof) made prior to the market crash of 2008. Not only did the industry fail to anticipate one of the biggest financial crises in history, many market strategists failed to predict the ensuing market rebound that took place following the collapse. And while market predictions at the end of 2011 warned us of the implosion of the bond market, the collapse of the Euro zone, and the death of equities, not one of these predictions came true.

Why are investment predictions so often wrong? There are several key reasons. For one, it is impossible to correctly predict the movement of an asset class without predicting the numerous factors that influence asset prices. Therefore, to predict asset class prices, strategists also need to be able to accurately predict the following: direction of the economy; supply and demand factors for the industry; interest rates; government, regulatory, and environmental constraints; and every possible future innovation. Good luck!

Take the complexity of innovations for example: five years ago, the predominant oil price predictions were based on the concept that the world had reached "peak oil"—the point in time when the global pro-duction of oil had reached its maximum rate, after which production would gradually decline forever and there would be no new discoveries of oil. Economists from high-profile Canadian and global institutions predicted that oil prices would reach $225 or more a barrel. In 2013, however, the price of a barrel of oil is $90. Economists and market strat-egists failed to accurately predict developments in technology. In the last five years, technological innovations have resulted in more effective drilling methods. These industry innovations (such as fracking) have allowed oil companies to tap into massive oil reserves. The jury is still out on exactly how this technology will be implemented and whether or not it is environmentally acceptable. However, as a result of these innovations, oil industry experts are now reversing their earlier predic-tions and some are even predicting—holy smokes!—that the U.S. will become the world's largest oil producer by 2017. This was an unthink-able concept just a few years ago, mainly because the people who earn a living making predictions were calling for just the opposite.

The financial industry wants you to believe that it can successfully predict future market outcomes; many investors eagerly buy into this notion, often with dangerous results. The truth is that *no one* can predict future asset prices. Making major portfolio bets on these predictions is one of the most dangerous things an investor can do.

The tendency to make predictions isn't unique to finance. Coverage of American college basketball's NCAA March Madness doesn't limit itself to reporting scores, it also devotes hours of pre-tournament programming to predicting the brackets. For those unfamiliar with March Madness, fans and experts alike try to pick the winner of every game at the beginning of the tournament. It is near impossible to accurately predict the entire bracket, yet hearing the basketball experts talk about it would lead you to believe that it is an exact science. This is especially telling when you take into account that some of the most accurate brackets in recent years were made by children who picked the winners based on how much they liked a team's jerseys. Say what you will, it's a much more honest and open system than the one used by the people who make market predictions.

The truth of the matter is that no one can consistently predict future asset prices. As seen in figure 3, markets and asset classes often move in a random and unpredictable fashion. Each colour represents a different asset class that is worthy of being included in a Canadian's investment portfolio. They are laid out year by year in a stacked format with the best performance within that calendar year on the top and the worst performance on the bottom. Investors often regret bold portfolio moves based on previous forecasts and predictions. Switching back and forth between various asset classes based on predictions is an unproductive and risky strategy.

Studying the People behind the Predictions

Investors should also be wary of market gurus who make their predictions with unshakeable confidence. David Dunning and other researchers have documented a troubling pattern: individuals who rank among the worst predictors tend to be the ones who have the most confidence in their abilities.

To test this troubling pattern, Dunning and his colleague Justin Kruger asked people to rate how they performed on a logic and reasoning

Figure 3: Attempting to Switch between Asset Classes is Unproductive and Risky

2000	2001	2002	2003	2004	2005	2006	2007	2008	2009	2010	2011	2012
36.18	24.88	2.58	36.10	23.47	24.11	35.72	9.82	2.56	68.35	38.09	11.72	15.08
28.30	21.56	2.39	31.32	22.49	21.44	29.88	4.27	-21.94	46.22	23.38	4.30	14.96
12.24	19.35	-3.63	30.11	17.53	19.56	26.10	3.36	-22.85	35.05	21.50	2.04	14.72
7.41	4.36	-3.79	27.83	15.28	10.97	26.08	2.15	-24.94	27.29	17.61	0.90	14.55
5.17	1.63	-3.86	26.74	14.47	10.95	23.18	-5.25	-25.55	25.12	16.40	-3.52	14.13
1.54	1.05	-12.45	18.85	11.49	10.72	22.11	-7.92	-30.06	13.99	14.53	-5.19	13.82
0.24	-6.40	-16.02	13.57	10.98	10.69	18.15	-10.09	-30.67	13.85	10.26	-8.71	13.04
-5.54	-11.56	-16.75	11.60	8.63	4.16	17.25	-10.14	-32.53	10.98	9.16	-10.00	11.68
-7.77	-12.57	-16.77	7.46	8.42	3.05	16.56	-15.63	-33.00	9.26	2.22	-10.26	7.19
-8.82	-13.41	-20.47	5.46	2.80	2.57	15.58	-17.01	-35.24	3.47	0.43	-12.43	0.91
-10.80	-16.55	-22.85	2.86	2.25	2.29	3.93	-29.73	-45.71	0.36	-2.14	-13.78	0.80

Legend:
Canadian Fixed Income
Canadian Large Cap
Canadian Value
Canadian Small Cap
US Large Cap
US Value
US Small Cap
US Real Estate
International Large Cap
International Value
International Small Cap

Source: Dimensional Fund Advisors

Figure 4: Unskilled and Unaware of It

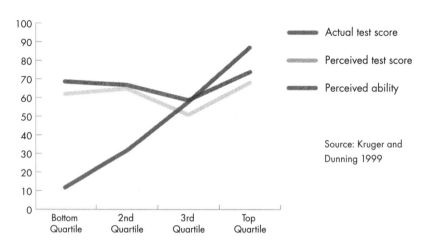

test.[1] Figure 4 splits the different ratings for perceived ability, perceived score, and actual score into the four quartiles based on performance. Remarkably, those who did not perform well still had very high levels of confidence in their perceived abilities. It's no wonder that we can get into difficulties by listening to market forecasters.

Philip Tetlock followed the views of experts on world politics for more than a decade.[2] He writes that, "Almost as many experts as not thought that the Soviet Communist Party would remain firmly in the saddle of power in 1993, that Canada was doomed by 1997, that neofascism would prevail in Pretoria by 1994, and that the [Economic and Monetary Union] would collapse by 1997." Tetlock found that, although these experts rated their confidence at 80% or higher, their predictions were correct no more than 45% of the time.

Why do market analysts continue to make predictions when they are so frequently wrong? Partly because it is in the interest of the financial services industry to appear to know what will happen in the future, and partly because investors take comfort in building investment portfolios around predictions.

Another factor may be that the people making the predictions have an effective arsenal of excuses for when they are wrong. Tetlock identified strategies frequently used by predictors to explain their errors. These include the "although the forecast was wrong, the analysis is still valid" defense; the "I was almost right" defense; and the "it just hasn't happened yet" defense. My personal favourite is the "if only" defense, as in: "If only the Central Bank had raised interest rates, then my forecast would have been accurate." Tetlock concluded that "expertise thus may not translate into predictive accuracy, but it does translate into the ability to generate explanations for predictions that experts themselves find compelling, resulting in massive overconfidence."

In truth, no one has the ability to consistently forecast important geopolitical and economic outcomes—there are no crystal balls. With catchphrases like "Ten Stocks to Buy Now" and "How to Retire Rich," the advice business has largely succeeded in convincing investors that it has the inside track. Predicting an uncertain future has become the bread and butter of many in the financial services industry, and the public has been all too willing to buy into it. In the short term, setting the entire direction of your portfolio on the basis of a few predictions may lead to joy or misery; in the long term, it might lead to much less than you'd hoped for—not to mention encouraging you to become that Nervous Nelly investor you never wanted to be.

Pitfall 8: Letting Behavioural Biases Get in the Way

Humans are not hardwired to be great investors. Emotions such as fear and greed often cloud our judgment and lead us to do things with our portfolios that we later regret. Our brains also have a set of filters—or thinking biases—that can lead us to make less than rational investment decisions.

Successful investors are aware of the impact emotions can have on portfolio decisions. Warren Buffett writes: "Success in investing doesn't correlate with I.Q. ... Once you have ordinary intelligence, what you need is the temperament to control the urges that get other people into trouble in investing." Unfortunately, few investors have Buffett's unflappable temperament. For the rest of us, money is an emotional subject, and the choices we make in the wake of an exciting stock tip or a plummeting portfolio affect our investment results in real and often damaging ways.

Behavioural finance is a relatively new field that attempts to better understand and explain how human emotions and cognitive errors influence investors and their decision-making processes. The research combines human psychology and the science of economics. This area has critical implications for your financial life: indeed, behaviour is far more important in determining investment success than any technical benchmarks.

So powerful and insightful are the findings from behavioural finance that one of the pioneers in this field, Daniel Kahneman, won the 2002 Nobel Prize in Economic Sciences. Kahneman's work (in collaboration with the late Amos Tversky) laid the foundation for a new field of research by discovering how human judgment may take shortcuts that lead to poor decision-making.

Some of the more common cognitive errors include:

Herding behaviour: being driven by a desire to be part of the crowd or by an assumption that the majority knows best.

Mental accounting: treating some money (such as gambling winnings or an unexpected bonus) differently than other money.

Availability bias: making decisions based on the information most readily available rather than considering all relevant information.

Loss aversion: a tendency to make decisions designed to avoid losses rather than to achieve gains.

Hindsight bias: the belief that a recent unexpected event could have been foreseen ("of course a financial crisis was going to occur in 2008—it was obvious"), which provides subconscious support to the belief that we can predict future outcomes.

Confirmation bias: the tendency to look for evidence and research that confirms our investment beliefs, while disregarding evidence and research that does not.

Home bias: the belief that investing in our own country is less risky because it is more familiar.

Confidence bias: over-confidence is the opposite of fear of loss and can be just as devastating to an investment portfolio. This behaviour results partly from the optimistic tendency of humans to unrealistically overrate our abilities.

Behavioural biases like these explain why very smart people still fall prey to classic investment pitfalls. It's not realistic to expect anyone to be immune to these biases: they are part of what makes us human. However, you can reduce the likelihood that they will detract from your investment decisions if you have a plan in place and the discipline to stick with it. Have you, your investment advisor, or your professional money manager ever been trapped by one or more of these behavioural biases? Chances are that you have.

Empower Yourself—Become Aware

Awareness pays off. Financial markets have been extremely challenging in the last decade and the 2008–2009 financial crisis was just the latest sharp edge that rattled investors into succumbing to one or more of the pitfalls. It is important for investors to learn from their past mistakes and focus on obtaining the best possible returns available to them. Investors must:

- become aware of pitfalls that can endanger their long-term investment success;

- educate themselves on capital markets and how they work, the relationship between risk and return, and the strategies to avoid common mistakes;
- build investment plans using time-tested strategies based on diversification and long-term asset allocation; and
- execute and maintain their chosen investment plan with discipline.

It's time for a different kind of investment strategy—one that allows investors to pursue their dreams without endangering their livelihoods. Education and awareness enable investors to see beyond market hype and empower them to make better decisions. A structured, well-executed portfolio is critical to producing a profitable and winning strategy for your investments.

2

The Emperor Has No Clothes

LEARN TO RECOGNIZE CONFLICTS OF INTEREST WITHIN THE FINANCIAL SERVICES INDUSTRY

To have a successful investment experience, we must thoroughly understand the obstacles that can prevent us from succeeding. In chapter 1, we learned about the pitfalls to which investors often succumb. A second challenge that may keep us from achieving long-term wealth is the prevalence of conflicts of interest within the investment advisory world.

Many advisors in the investment industry are conscientious professionals who strive to provide the best possible advice and service to their clients. However, the way the system operates can lead advisors and firms to place their own interests ahead of their clients. Investors can avoid frustration and anxiety by becoming aware of these conflicts and learning to recognize and identify them appropriately.

While these conflicts are as old as the market, the abuses investors witnessed over the last decade have shone a much-needed light on some of the industry's most questionable (but not uncommon) practices. The strong performance of equity bull markets in the 1980s and 1990s was enough to mask internal conflicts within the industry. The cracks in the system only started to become visible to many investors during the long period of lower returns that we have experienced since 2000, a period that included two investment storms: the bear market of 2002 and the credit crisis of 2008–2009. These recent experiences, combined with the revelations of the last ten years, have led investors to be skeptical with regard to both how their money is being managed and the people managing it. This skepticism is perfectly healthy; I encourage all investors to adopt it in their dealings with the sales-driven segment of the financial industry. Remember, the best way to know if your advisor has all the right answers is to ask the right questions. It's your money; the more you understand how this business works, the better you'll be at taking care of it.

Let us begin with a quick review of the events of the last ten years:

- Corporate executives were paid exorbitant bonuses while the companies they managed failed to meet expectations. Early in the decade, we saw abuses at senior executive levels at firms such as Nortel, WorldCom, Tyco, and Enron. After the 2008–2009 credit crisis, we experienced firsthand the greed of Wall Street, the investment banking community, and the U.S. real estate mortgage industry. Senior executives at various levels of the mortgage-selling process lined their pockets while selling toxic loans to unsuspecting investors.
- Wall Street and Bay Street brokerage research analysts have been found guilty of overrating the value of the stocks they suggested and recommended.
- The Canadian mutual fund industry has been called out for their high fees and low service offerings.
- The hedge fund industry has also been called out for their outrageous fees and has been under fire for misconduct.
- Ponzi schemes and outright theft— costing investors billions of dollars that will never be recovered—were exposed as multiple cases came to light.

The greed of the players involved—the big shooters and the deal-makers —has encouraged gross mismanagement and fuelled criminal activities designed to dupe investors. The sheer volume of headlines, trials, and investigations is enough to make us cynical and desensitized, but we should remember that, for every imprisoned executive, there are countless ordinary people who lost real money. Retirement accounts, savings for education, financing to start a dream business—

these things and more were lost because of the greed of professionals in the financial industry.

How does this happen? Even after major events like the collapse of 2008–2009, the majority of investors remain unaware that the financial services industry is built on a number of critical conflicts of interest.

Investors can make sense of corruption at the executive level. However, it is much more challenging for ordinary investors to identify and understand the subtle conflicts of interest embedded within the day-to-day services of Canadian financial services firms. These firms spend a fortune on slick marketing campaigns that invariably hide any questionable dealings and focus the spotlight on spectacular (and often mythical) returns. These conflicts are especially well-hidden even to the most astute investors.

Government Report Reveals Conflicts of Interest

There has long been considerable debate over how investment advisors are paid. It was a key focus of two reports released in the 1990s by former Ontario Securities Commissioner Glorianne Stromberg for the Office of Consumer Affairs.[1] Although now dated, her controversial reports focused attention on lesser-known aspects of the investment funds industry, including self-regulation, sales practices and incentive schemes, conflicts of interest, gaps in consumer and industry education, fund governance issues, and problems with the disclosure system. While the reports served as a wake-up call to many in the financial world, they unfortunately reached few investors.

There has been some good news lately. In 2012, the Canadian Securities Administrators (CSA) established a series of industry guidelines (similar to a code of conduct) known as the Client Relationship Model (CRM). The CRM's goal is based on three core principles: increased transparency regarding the relationship between the client, the service provider, and the firm; transparency regarding the investor's account performance along with the cost of managing the account; and disclosure of conflicts of interest. The CRM is intended to enhance the advisor/client relationship by clearly delineating the roles and responsibilities of the investment professional towards his or her client. As a result, advisors and dealers will be required to enact greater disclosure regimes and higher standards of product suitability over the next two years. The CSA is hoping that the code of conduct will better protect investors by making them more aware of the overall performance of their investments and the value of the services they receive relative to the costs associated with the wealth management services rendered. The CRM will be implemented in several stages over the next few years.

However, the newly-adopted CRM philosophy alone cannot protect investors from the embedded conflicts of interest in the day-to-day operations of the financial industry. Investors need to take it upon themselves to become better educated and more savvy in selecting their advisory firm and in their dealings with the industry at large.

Conflicts in Financial Advice

Where are the conflicts of interest? Why do they exist? How do you identify them? Unlike many other independent advice-providing professions (lawyers, accountants, architects, engineers etc.), the financial advice business, is filled with questionable selling practices. Because the creators of financial products (such as mutual funds, IPOs, and proprietary in-house products) frequently pay advisors to distribute and sell on their behalf, questions naturally arise as to the independence of that advice.

The investment advice business is like no other. Smooth marketing campaigns and the sure-fire tips of industry "experts" are designed to make us believe that your financial well-being is their number one priority. Unfortunately, the investment industry does not make a profit simply by ensuring that your financial wealth is intact; it makes money by selling you products and strategies. As we shall see, some of these products do more harm than good. It's difficult to imagine the practices of the financial sector in any other industry, because they would never be allowed to operate in such a way. Imagine if you hired a nutritionist to advise you on what foods and supplements you should be consuming as part of a healthy diet. You believe that you've hired a trained professional whose top priority is your well-being. Yet what if your nutritionist advised you to consume certain supplements, not because they would benefit you, but because the supplement manufacturers were paying your nutritionist to promote or sell their products. Even worse, what if these same companies were actually paying commissions to your nutritionist for switching or trading your supplements from one brand to another, regardless of their benefits. Knowing this, would you be confident that your diet is really what's best for you? Welcome to the world of sales-driven investment advice.

Conflicts in the Brokerage Industry

Stock analysts work in a world rife with competing pressures, and clients often find themselves on the losing side of this equation. According to a study conducted at the University of Michigan's business school, brokerage firm analysts often provide biased research in response to investment banking pressures. "Sell-side analysts have long faced allegations that pressures to generate investment banking business compromise the soundness of their investment research," says Richard Sloan, professor of accounting and finance at the University of Michigan. "Our evidence supports these allegations. We found that analysts routinely hype the stock of firms raising new financing so that these firms can issue securities at temporarily inflated prices."[2]

At the heart of the conflict are the investment-banking relationships that brokerage firms have with issuing companies. When companies issue new securities, they hire investment bankers within brokerage firms for advice on structuring the deal as well as for the eventual sale and distribution of the new securities to investors. Brokerage firms often generate more revenue by underwriting a company's securities offerings and providing other investment banking services. These IPOs or secondary offerings are highly lucrative for the firms and their sales force of brokers; the investments often end up being stuffed in private client accounts. Providing an independent and unbiased private investor service for all investors becomes impossible when these revenue opportunities get in the way. The broker and the brokerage firms are torn between doing the right thing for clients and generating the most revenue for themselves. Yet what is best for the brokerage firms and banks may not be best for their clients. When the interests fail to align, the ordinary investor always loses.

Aside from being a dishonest abuse of retail clients, this practice of scratching each other's backs has staggering consequences in the markets. The credit crisis of 2008–2009 was caused in part by the new issue creation and distribution of toxic loans and assets by banks and brokerage houses. Surely there should have been scores of analysts who could have sounded the warning bells and identified the risks that were being taken in the years leading up to the crisis? After the crash, many analysts spoke of the poor offerings and the less-than-adequate due-diligence process used to bring so much of this rubbish to market. So why did they do it to begin with? Greed, money, and conflicts of interests ruled the day.

The 2008–2009 credit crisis is a fairly extreme case that teaches us about the rigged system and the conflicts that hamper unbiased investment advice within the brokerage industry. Every week of the year, Canadian brokerage firms bring to market commission-based IPOs and new product offerings, thereby creating conflicts for their investment advisors to manage and making it difficult for those advisors to provide sound, unbiased investment advice to their clients.

Conflicts in the Mutual Fund Industry

The invention of the mutual fund was a remarkable feat. Prior to the 1920s, only the truly wealthy in the United States had access to services that could diversify their equity positions. On 21 March 1924, the first official mutual fund in North America—the Massachusetts Investors Trust—was born. The mutual fund structure allowed everyone to buy into equity markets in a diversified fashion, an amazing innovation that launched a democratization process giving investors real access to capital markets.

Something changed in the early to mid-1990s. With the explosive growth of the mutual fund industry and the sheer size of its assets came the polished marketing campaigns, the radio, print, and T V commercials, and the questionable sales practices.

In recent years, much has been written about the mutual fund industry's outlandish fees, over-diversification, below-average performance, short-term thinking, and aggressive sales practices. "Right now the average annual expense ratio in the United States for a mutual fund is about 1.3%, but when you add trading costs and all the other fees, you can get up to 3% in annual costs," says Gary Gensler, former undersecretary of the United States Treasury and co-author of 2002's *The Great Mutual Fund Trap*. At the time of his report, Gensler calculated the following annual costs for U.S. mutual funds: management fees (1.3%), lost earnings on cash holdings (0.25%), higher taxes due to all the short-term trading (1% or more), and trading commission costs brought on by high churn within funds (0.5 to 1%).

In Canada, our annual expense ratios are much higher than those of our American counterparts. The average Canadian equity fund has an annual expense ratio hovering around 2.5%. Part of the fee discrepancy between Canadian and U.S. funds is explained by higher embedded advisor trailer fees paid to Canadian advisors. American advisors often charge their fees independently from the underlying funds; thus, advisory fees and services are closely linked. In Canada, unfortunately, the embedded fee is often misunderstood and subjects the client to the possibility of a very low service promise. Canadian mutual fund investors often do not realize that they are owed a service in return for paying the higher fee.

More disturbing is the Canadian mutual fund advisors' penchant for selling funds via the deferred service charge (DSC) model. The DSC creates a large up-front commission payment to the advisor and, in return, locks the investor into the mutual fund for up to seven years. The problem with the DSC is that it encourages advisors to always be looking for "new clients" and "new assets" rather than servicing existing clients. The DSC might also encourage advisors to move funds around within an existing client account in order to trigger more DSC commission payments to the advisor and reload the client portfolio with longer penalty exits. This practice, called "churning," is unethical and is one of the unruly sales practices noted in the 1990s by the Ontario Securities Commissioner Glorianne Stromberg and the Office of Consumer Affairs.

This is not to say that the entire mutual fund industry is offside. There are many reputable Canadian investment management firms and financial advisors who responsibly manage and use mutual funds for their clients. These financial advisors provide their clients with valuable wealth management services. The challenge for investors lies in coping with the selling practices and marketing hype of retail sales–driven financial organizations which, unfortunately, tend by their very nature to be the most visible players in the Canadian mutual fund industry.

Rethinking Investment Advice

These ongoing problems are a disheartening sign that individual investors still suffer from a rigged system. Empowering investors is the process of sharing information and allowing investors to take control of their investment plans and their wealth destiny. Education about the challenges faced by all investors with respect to conflicts of interest in the financial services industry is an important first step in the journey towards a successful investment experience. If anything, the negative attention of the last decade has prompted change. The CSA's new proposals are designed to illuminate the industry's conflicts. Investors are becoming increasingly aware of these conflicts and demanding a higher standard from Canada's investment industry. As baby-boomers, the media, and other voices call for improved transparency and integrity, positive changes are occurring within the industry. By successfully avoiding investment pitfalls and navigating industry conflicts, you can greatly increase your odds of attaining investment success.

The good news is that you don't need a crystal ball to have a good investment experience. Time-tested, winning strategies do exist—investment plans that are based not on any predictive fallacies nor on hype or luck but on superior evidence-based research that brings structure and discipline to money and wealth management. Discovered fifty years ago, these proven investment management strategies have been used for decades by institutional investors, foundations, and wealthy families. In addition, recent research on the measurable and identifiable factors that drive portfolio performance can enhance your understanding of capital markets and their role in your investment portfolio, allowing you to make better investment decisions.

What does redefining investment advice mean? It means changing the rules of the game. It means getting investment advice that is based on building, monitoring, and bringing order to the portfolio management process. It means accessing the type of investment solutions that were once reserved only for the most serious market—the institutional pension funds. Investors must understand the dos and don'ts of money management, recognize the key factors, and know how to avoid the classic investment pitfalls. The new breed of evidence-based investment advice does not make grandiose promises of spectacular returns and it discourages chasing the flavour of the month. It is a system based on integrity and evidence: a system that empowers the investor.

Time-tested, successful solutions *do* exist—as does a growing list of conflict-free consultants and advisory firms in Canada who provide independent investment recommendations without charging commissions. Becoming an *empowered investor* is less complicated than you might think. Read on to find the blueprint for your financial success.

3

Invest in Asset Classes

PORTFOLIO STRUCTURE DETERMINES PERFORMANCE

Having reviewed the pitfalls that can catch the unwary investor, as well as conflicts of interest within the industry at large, we can now turn to some concrete solutions. The next chapters deal with a series of winning principles that set the foundation for successful long-term investing. Understanding these principles is a crucial first step to ensuring the safety of your financial future. In doing so, we will be casting off the fast-food philosophy that can affect many of our most important investment decisions.

There are three types of investing: market timing, stock picking, and asset class investing. Market timing and stock picking are based on the belief that someone can either predict the future or gain by analyzing the errors of others. Wall Street and Bay Street firms spend billions of dollars trying to convince investors that it is possible to out-predict the competition.

Stock picking is an attempt to identify winning stocks and presumes that someone—whether you, your advisor, or the newest guru—can consistently find under-priced securities that others have failed to discover. Market timing presumes that someone can *consistently* identify when the entire market or a market sector is over- or under-priced and buy or sell equities accordingly. Successful stock picking and market timing entail the accurate prediction of future geopolitical, economic, financial, or technological events and advances. Because it is nearly

Figure 5: Portfolio Structure and Asset Allocation Determine Performance

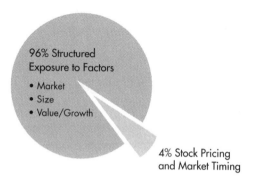

96% Structured
Exposure to Factors

- Market
- Size
- Value/Growth

4% Stock Pricing
and Market Timing

Source: Dimensional Fund Advisors

impossible to make such predictions, both stock picking and market timing are fuelled by hype and prey on emotion rather than reason.

Asset class investing, on the other hand, is all about putting your eggs into many different baskets. It is the process of distributing and diversifying wealth in different asset classes, most typically in various types of stocks, bonds, cash, and other alternatives. Asset class investing provides insurance against things going wrong in one investment class— as is likely to occur from time to time. Ideally, your investments should be as diversified as possible; this will afford you a steady increase over time and protect your investments from the constant fluctuations of a single kind of security. Asset class investing is a much more prudent way to invest than either stock picking or market timing.

Even though stock-picking and market-timing forecasts grab all the headlines in the daily business newspapers and the nightly TV investment shows, research demonstrates that asset class investing is by far the most important factor in determining the variability or movement of your overall portfolio. Studies have demonstrated that asset class returns may account for up to 96% of the variation of portfolio returns.[1] Figure 5 highlights the results of a study that compared returns from a large number of different institutional portfolios and proved that the difference in variation between portfolios could mainly be explained by three primary asset allocation portfolio weightings: equity markets vs. bonds; small company stocks vs. large company stocks; and value company stocks vs. growth company stocks. Stock picking and market timing accounted for only 4% of the variation.

Asset Class Investing is the Healthy Alternative

Asset class investing is the most important step you can take to ensure the success of your portfolio. While it is not as sexy as stock picking or market timing, the proof is in the numbers. If stock picking and market timing are the fast-food, feel-good fix of the investment universe, asset class investing is the healthy alternative that will ensure your long-term financial well-being. Also known as asset allocation or portfolio diversification, asset class investing is one of the fundamental principles of modern portfolio theory. This ground-breaking scientific theory, which will be further discussed in chapter 4, was developed by Harry Markowitz and William Sharpe, who won the Nobel Prize for economics in 1990.[2]

Asset allocation is an established method of investing. Institutional pools of capital have used this methodology for decades and over the past twenty years it has been described in scores of articles in newspapers and specialized publications. Despite this wide media coverage, however, the methodology is often underused or misapplied by investors. Investors may buy into asset allocation strategies only to later find themselves deviating from them by falling prey to the emotions and investment biases discussed in chapter 1. Although nothing in the markets is ever guaranteed, the principle of asset allocation can profoundly shift the odds in an investor's favour.

This investing philosophy has been successfully implemented by wealthy families and the pension funds of nearly all of Canada's largest companies and major universities—the only difference between those investors and you is knowledge of these strategies. In reading thus far, you have made the choice to become an *empowered investor*. From this point on, the time you spend reading this book could change the way you invest forever.

4

Diversify

DIVERSIFY YOUR WEALTH AMONG
DIFFERENT ASSET CLASSES

Most North Americans know that portfolio diversification is important. We all want to be diversified—as long as we are diversified in the top ten funds in the two hottest sectors or in ten individual stocks that all have positive returns.

It's human nature to think this way. It was also the prevalent method of investing in the early 1900s. In fact, right up until the mid-1950s, most leading investment guides recommended that investors find a few individual stocks with the highest expected returns and invest in them while ignoring all other factors.

In the mid-1950s, a young graduate student at the University of Chicago named Harry Markowitz dared to think differently. He believed that investors should be equally as concerned with the risks or volatility of their investments as they were with the returns. Markowitz's conclusions launched a movement that changed the way people thought about investing. To this day, many serious pension funds and endowments include this tenet in their investment approach.

The Simple Beauty of Portfolio Theory

To create a successful investment experience, investors need to understand the importance of portfolio theory. Markowitz concluded that:

- Diversifying across different asset classes reduces portfolio risk.

- Combining asset classes that do not behave alike will improve the returns of the entire portfolio.

What is remarkable about Markowitz's discovery is that it allows an investor to control the volatility of a portfolio and increase its return at the same time. His landmark contribution to portfolio management hinged on the important discovery that, by combining asset classes that have good long-term prospects but *behave differently*, investors can achieve better returns with less risk. So how do we define "asset classes that behave differently"? Markowitz defined this relationship as an inverse correlation. In layman's terms, this means asset classes that are not always in sync with one another and that may sometimes even move in opposite directions.

You can see a perfect example of asset classes that behave differently by reviewing your personal net worth statement for the period from 2000 to 2013. Compare your investment statements that held globally-diversified equities to the value of your personal residence. Each is an asset class with good long-term prospects; however, they are not in sync with one another. If you compare the movement of your stock portfolio with the movement in price of your real estate holdings (home, cottage, etc.), you will see that their values did not move together. Holding these two asset classes between 2000 and 2013 would have had an interesting effect on your personal balance sheet: while your global stock portfolio may have limped along, your home, cottage, or investment property probably saw significant appreciation thanks to the boom in Canadian real estate. By contrast, throughout the 1990s, in the same two asset classes, the complete opposite occurred, with global stock values increasing and Canadian real estate values dropping. By maintaining a diversified personal balance sheet between 1990 and 2013, you would have experienced the benefits of diversification.

The Benefits of Implementing Portfolio Theory

Applying portfolio theory to your investments has both scientific and personal benefits. Scientifically, portfolio theory offers improved risk/

return ratios; in other words, you will achieve better rates of return for each unit of risk that you are willing to take. The personal benefits are just as powerful for individual investors. A diversified and structured approach to portfolio construction protects investors from many of the classic investment pitfalls and from the potential for capital destruction created by chasing hot or trendy investment ideas. This protection alone is a powerful incentive for individual investors to adopt and use the diversification approach. Portfolio theory allows investors to bring structure and logic to their investment experience.

When carefully thought through, this elegant yet remarkable investment concept has multiple benefits:

- it can protect investors from common investment pitfalls (chapter 1);
- it builds better rates of return per unit of risk;
- it increases the investor's ability to preserve capital; and
- it affords investors peace of mind compared to the ups and downs of traditional performance-chasing investing.

Figure 6 demonstrates the quantitative benefits of portfolio theory. Portfolio 1 represents a typical single asset class strategy with all capital invested in Canadian stocks only. Portfolios 2, 3, and 4 show the addition of different percentages of non-correlated equity asset classes. Adding these new asset classes into each subsequent portfolio has an impressive outcome: an increase in the rates of return and a decrease in overall risk (as measured by standard deviation). Portfolio 4 generated a higher annualized return—1.38% more in absolute terms —than Portfolio 1 with less volatility. Assuming a starting investment of $10,000 in January 1982, Portfolio 4 generated $70,500 more funds over this period than Portfolio 1.

It is important to remember that these are historical numbers (1982 to 2012) and should not be viewed as projections of future rates of return for various asset class combinations. To build a portfolio you can live with, you need to focus on forward-looking expected rates of return, volatilities, and correlations of various asset classes.

Figure 6: The Benefits of Portfolio Theory

Portfolio	1	2	3	4

ASSET CLASS[1]				
Canadian Large Companies	100%	33.4%	30%	30%
U.S. Large Companies		33.3%	30%	10%
U.S. Value Companies				10%
U.S. Small Companies				10%
Int'l Large Companies		33.3%	30%	10%
Int'l Value Companies				10%
Int'l Small Companies				10%
U.S. REITs			10%	10%
Total	100%	100%	100%	100%
Annualized return	9.06%	9.70%	9.88%	10.44%
Standard deviation	15.53%	12.81%	12.37%	12.37%
Growth of $10,000	$146,900	$176,600	$185,600	$217,400

These portfolios do not represent suggested or recommended allocations but are merely examples used to demonstrate the effects and benefits of portfolio diversification.
31 January 1982 to 31 December 2012, returns in Canadian dollars.

To fully grasp the benefits of diversification, you need to understand what is happening at the asset class or building-block level. By comparing the characteristics (returns and volatility) of asset classes within a portfolio to the overall portfolio, you get a better understanding of the impact and the benefits of combining non-correlated asset classes. To demonstrate this, table 3 reviews the result of a simple model portfolio that incorporates two asset classes.

Portfolios A and B (one asset class per portfolio) each generated historic returns and degrees of volatility that would be entirely accept-

Table 3: The Benefits of Combining Asset Classes

	Return	Volatility	Unit of Volatility ÷ Unit of Return
Portfolio A 1 single asset class 100% Canadian Equity	9.06%	15.53%	1.72
Portfolio B 1 single asset class 100% International Equity	8.5%	15.80%	1.86
Portfolio C Combination of 2 asset classes 50% Canadian Equity 50% International Equity	9.11%	13.66%	1.50

Source: Canadian and International Equity are represented by the TSX/S&P Composite Index and MSCI EAFE Index, 31 January 1982 to 31 December 2012, returns in Canadian dollars.

able outcomes in and of themselves. But can we do better? What if we decided to combine these two portfolios? How will they react together? This brings us to the concept of correlation between asset classes.

Correlation measures the degree to which two securities (or asset classes) move in similar patterns. Correlation values range from -1.0 (which indicates that the two securities moved in perfect opposition to each other) to 1.0 (which indicates that the two asset classes moved perfectly in tandem). You can calculate correlation measures between any two asset classes. If the correlation between two asset classes is less than 1, diversification benefits exist. In most cases the correlation between traditional asset classes is positive but less than 1.

In the example in table 3, the actual correlation between large Canadian stocks (measured by the S&P/TSX Composite Index) and international stocks (measured by the MSCI EAFE Index) was 0.49 for this period. This means that the asset classes were not always going up and down together in perfect sync. When you combine the two classes to create a new portfolio—Portfolio C—the volatility of Portfolio C is more favourable than that of either Portfolio A or B. Any rational investor would prefer Portfolio C since it generated a similar, in fact slightly better, return at a lower level of volatility: or, in human terms, more gain for less pain.

What is amazing about these research findings is that the benefits of this strategy are available to all investors—large or small, it doesn't matter—everywhere in the world. Very few things in the investment world are free for the taking; the benefit of diversifying your asset classes, however, is one of them.

Choosing Your Asset Classes

The choice of which asset classes to include in your portfolio is critical. This decision will drive the vast majority of your returns. What should you look for when choosing asset classes? Search for asset classes that have good long-term expected returns per unit of risk and, if possible, choose those that have less than perfect correlations to each other. This will allow the benefits of diversification to materialize.

As discussed in the opening chapter, most investors know that it's prudent to diversify, but do they truly practice diversification in their portfolios? Many people who believe they are well diversified actually have highly concentrated and risky portfolios. Investors often discover that their portfolios are filled with overlapping strategies resulting in poor asset class diversification. Good asset class diversification occurs when many distinct and productive asset classes are added together to build an effective long-term portfolio strategy.

When reviewing potential candidates to include in a diversified portfolio, Canadian investors should consider the following asset classes:

Fixed Income:
* Canadian government and corporate bonds
* Real return bonds

Revenue Investments:
* Canadian and global real estate investment trusts (REITs)

Figure 7: Poor Asset Class Diversification vs. Good Asset Class Diversification

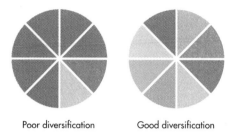

Poor diversification   Good diversification

Equity:
- Canadian large companies
- Canadian value companies
- Canadian small companies
- U.S. large companies
- U.S. value companies
- U.S. small companies
- International large companies
- International value companies
- International small companies
- Emerging market companies

As we will learn later in the book, investors also have much to gain by diversifying and including such various factors as small companies, value companies, and highly profitable companies—also known as the small cap, value, and profitability factors.

With its tenet that asset allocation is a key strategy in any successful investment framework, portfolio theory should be the financial blueprint of choice for most Canadian investors. In chapter 5, we will examine the ground-breaking research that builds on this strategy and that can further improve your odds of investment success.

5

Choose Your Investment Tools Wisely

DISCOVER THE POWER OF INDEX-BASED, ASSET CLASS INVESTMENT TOOLS

The great leaders of organizations, from the CEOs of multinational corporations to the coaches of winning sports franchises, all agree on one very important principle when it comes to achieving winning results: the success of their plans depends on the perfect execution of the smallest details.

The same principle applies to the world of investment management, where the devil is very much in the details. The methods we use to execute and implement our portfolio strategies go a long way towards ensuring our success. The next few chapters are devoted to the discussion of portfolio management execution issues.

Just as gourmet chefs seek out the choicest ingredients for their recipes, empowered investors are also in search of the best tools to build, execute, and monitor their investment plans founded on three key investment principles: Invest in Asset Classes (chapter 3) + Diversify (chapter 4) + Discover the Fama/French Three-Factor Model (to be discussed in chapter 8). Executing the investment strategy with the best investments possible is fundamental in the quest to create a successful investment experience.

Choosing Your Asset Class Investment Tools

Once you have decided to diversify your portfolio with multiple asset classes, the next step is to decide which investment vehicles will enable you to best capture the long-term expected returns of each asset class.

Your choices for executing an investment plan built on diversified asset class exposure are as follows:

- Selecting individual stocks (stock picking) for each asset class;
- Hiring an active investment manager. An active manager buys and sells securities, usually within a mutual fund or pooled/segregated investment, providing exposure to an asset class; or
- Using index-based or passively-managed asset class investment tools to provide exposure to each asset class.

We've already established that 96% of returns are the direct result of your asset class and risk-factor choices (not stock picking or market timing). In addition, your tools of choice should deliver transparency, tax-efficiency, and have minimal asset class performance drift. Above all, your investment tools must deliver solid long-term performance.

Empowered by Precise Index-Based or Passively-Managed Asset Class Investment Tools

The past fifteen years have witnessed impressive growth and innovation in index-based or passively-managed investment solutions for individual Canadian investors. Index-based or passively-managed asset class investment tools can be defined as an investment that holds a diversified basket of securities (either stocks or bonds) that track a commercial benchmark or, alternatively, represent the entire asset class.

In the 1980s and early 1990s, individual investors or advisors who wanted to capture an asset class return needed to hire the services of an active manager or otherwise choose a selection of stocks with their advisor to try to capture the returns of the asset class. With access to these index-based or passively-managed investment solutions, investors finally have viable and effective alternatives to active management. Access to these types of asset class investment tools and all the benefits that go with them embody the potential of empowered investing.

The two best types of index-based and passively-managed asset class investment tools available to Canadian investors are Exchange Traded Funds and DFA Asset Class Funds:

Exchange Traded Funds (ETFs): ETFs are manufactured and managed by institutional money managers such as Blackrock Inc., the Vanguard Group, State Street Global Advisors, or BMO Asset Management Inc. As of 31 December 2012, close to 275 ETFs were trading on the TSX, with many more trading on the U.S. exchanges. Index-based asset class investment tools such as ETFs track specific asset classes and have revolutionized the way portfolios can be created and constructed. ETFs track commercial indexes such as the S&P/TSX Composite Index, the S&P 500 Index, the MSCI EAFE Index, the MSCI Emerging Market Index, and a variety of Canadian bond market indices.

Exchange Traded Funds typically have management expense ratios (MERs) ranging from 0.09% to 0.69% (for more information, visit www.ishares.ca, www.vanguardcanada.ca, or www.etfs.bmo.com).

DFA Asset Class Funds: Dimensional Fund Advisors (DFA) is an institutional money manager headquartered in Austin, Texas. As of 31 December 2012, nine main Dimensional passively-managed funds were available to Canadian investors. Dimensional's passively-managed asset class funds do not track commercial indexes, nor do they have managers trying to actively pick and choose the next winners. Their asset class strategies capture factor exposures, such as value and small companies (capturing factor exposures will be discussed in greater detail in chapter 8). Dimensional Fund Advisors have provided institutions with these passively-managed strategies since 1981 and have a tremendous reputation for their index- and factor-based research.

Dimensional's asset class funds have MERs ranging from 0.38% to 0.80% on their F-Class strategies (for more information, visit www.dfacanada.com). Canadian investors wishing to invest in

DFA asset class strategies must work with and engage the services of a DFA-approved Canadian advisor or advisory firm.

If you use a financial advisor or portfolio manager to assist you with the ongoing management of your portfolio and your financial affairs, you will have to pay an advisory or portfolio management fee in addition to the ETF- or DFA-fund MERs. Fees for the services of a financial advisor or portfolio manager can average between 0.5% and 1.5%, depending on the size of your portfolio and the services rendered by the advisor or advisory firm.

Evolution of Index-Based and Passively-Managed Asset Class Investment Tools

Index-based or passive management—as opposed to active management—is not a new phenomenon. An index-based or passively-managed fund comes in the form of a pooled investment vehicle (usually a mutual fund but it can also be an ETF) that aims to replicate the movements of the commercial index through a set of rules of ownership that are held constant, regardless of market conditions.

Fifteen years ago, if a Canadian investor wanted to get exposure to U.S. and international companies, there were very few options available. At the time, only Canadian institutional accounts had the size and thus the buying power to gain access to institutional managers with expertise in investing in international companies. The only real choice open to non-institutional investors was a limited selection of expensive mutual-fund or brokerage-firm WRAP programs with MERs in the range of 2.5% to 3.0%. Even Canada's investment counsellor community (which served Canada's affluent) did not necessarily have the in-house expertise—or, for that matter, an investment option—to provide their clients with exposure to international equities.

Today, Canadian investors, advisors, and portfolio managers have access to a wide variety of low-fee, tax-efficient, and transparent asset class investment tools designed to capture the return of Canadian, U.S., International, and Emerging Markets asset classes and markets.

These new asset class investment tools are empowering and democratic. The next chapter will demonstrate why you should consider using these tools to capture the asset class returns in your diversified portfolio and debunk some of the myths surrounding their use.

6

Learn How Index or Passive Management Outperforms Active Management

MUTUAL FUNDS AND STOCK-PICKING INVESTMENT COUNSELLORS ARE NO LONGER SACRED COWS

"Picking stocks is hard, picking managers to pick stocks is hard, and picking the right managers at the right time to pick the right stocks is even harder."
From an AQR Capital Management white paper entitled *Building a Better Core Equity Portfolio*, May 2013 by Ronen Israel and Dan Villalon

It took the bear market of 2000–2002 for many investors to begin questioning the merits of stock-picking mutual funds and investment counsellors. We were led to believe that active stock-picking strategies would clobber asset class indexing strategies in a declining market. We were told that smart managers knew just how much cash to hold onto and which stocks to sell in the bear market, thus protecting investors from declines in equities. The credit crisis of 2008–2009 and the overall investing challenges of the last decade have further prompted investors to question the capabilities of active stock pickers. This skepticism has proven correct, as evidence has shown that the average active manager did not perform any better than the broad benchmarks against which they are measured.

The Origins and Early History of Indexing

The origins of index investing can be traced to members of the academic and institutional communities who discovered and developed the first index-based investment solutions. Economists cite the efficient-market hypothesis (EMH) when they justify the use of index funds. Professor Eugene Fama developed the EMH at the University of Chicago Booth School of Business in the early 1960s. It states that fund managers and stock analysts are constantly on the lookout for securities that will out-perform the market and that this competition is so effective that any new information about a company is immediately reflected in its stock prices. This makes it very difficult for investors, given the limited infor-mation available to them, to find incorrectly-priced stocks. An index fund aims to avoid the inefficiencies associated with stock selection. This conceptual thinking was the foundation on which the first index/passive managers built their strategies in the 1970s. Eugene Fama would go on to win the Nobel Prize in economics in 2013 for his work on the efficient market hypothesis.

In 1971, Jeremy Grantham and Dean LeBaron of Batterymarch Financial Management pitched their idea of an index investing strat-egy for institutional pension funds. The idea was elegant in its simpli-city: create an investment made up of the entire market. The companies and their respective weightings would be identical to the established index or benchmark. The fund would charge low fees to its investors because it would not need to hire entire departments of stock analysts and active portfolio managers. It would take two more years for Gran-tham and LeBaron to attract their first investors. When they did get their fund off the ground, they were given the "Dubious Achievement Award" from *Pensions & Investments Magazine*. Clearly there were many in the industry who remained skeptical.

In 1973, John McQuown and David G. Booth of Wells Fargo and Rex Sinquefield of American National Bank (the three would eventu-ally meet again at Dimensional Fund Advisors) founded the first S&P Composite Index Fund for institutional clients. At this point, all index strategies were reserved for institutional investors, many of whom were located in the United States.

Also in 1973, Burton Malkiel's influential book, *A Random Walk Down Wall Street*, rocked the world of retail investing. Presenting aca-demia's findings to the public in an easily understandable way, Malkiel sought to address the fact that most mutual funds failed to beat the market indices. He wrote:

> What we need is a no-load, minimum management-fee mutual fund that simply buys the hundreds of stocks making up the broad stock-market averages and does not trade from security to security in an attempt to catch the winners. Whenever below-average performance on the part of any mutual fund is noticed, fund spokesmen are quick to point out "You can't buy the averages."

Malkiel believed it was time the public could.

Index pioneer John Bogle answered Malkiel's call. A graduate of Princeton University, Bogle based his senior thesis on the theory that active mutual fund managers could make no claims to superior performance over the broad market averages. Bogle eventually founded the First Index Investment Trust, the first index fund available to individual investors, in 1975. Initial competitors heavily derided Bogle's First Index Investment Trust, claiming it was "un-American," and the majority of the investment industry dubbed it "Bogle's folly." Insiders refused to believe that investors would buy into a system that only delivered average market returns. But investors did—and the rest is history. Today, Vanguard manages approximately $2.5 trillion in assets. Investor-friendly indexed/passive management investment strategies are the key to long-term investment success.

The pioneers of index investing only really began to gain momentum in the 1980s. Vanguard, Dimensional Fund Advisors, State Street Global Advisors, and Wells Fargo (which eventually became Barclay's Global Investors and then Blackrock Inc., the manager of iShares) were the four institutional firms that revolutionized the index/passive industry and made it what it is today.

It's difficult to comprehend just how much these pioneers would change the game of finance. When we picture the great revolutions of the last century, we tend to focus on tangible shifts like the implementation of the assembly line and the invention of the personal computer. The men discussed above are to finance what Henry Ford, Bill Gates, and Steve Jobs are to their respective fields. They forever changed the way their industry operated. Just as there were those who doubted that every household would one day own a car and a computer, there were those who questioned the benefits of index investing. Such doubts continue to exist today. As you might expect, many of the doubters are those whose jobs are most threatened by the adoption of index-based strategies: financial institutions and active managers. However, the continued adoption of these strategies by new investors is a testament to the fact that investors and advisory firms around the world are embracing the benefits that come with this empowered approach to investing.

Table 4 lists a number of the core asset classes available to Canadian investors through Canadian mutual fund offerings and compares their returns to index and exchange-traded fund returns. This ten-year chart covers an interesting period, including the recovery following the 2000–2002 bear market and the full effects of the credit crisis of 2008–2009. The extreme market movements of the recent credit crisis should have provided ample opportunity for the Canadian mutual fund industry to showcase the merits of active management. Unfortunately for the active-management community, the returns in ALL major asset classes demonstrate that Canadian investors would have been better off investing in index-based alternatives rather than in actively-managed funds.

Beware of Survivorship Biases in "Median Manager Averages"

Unfortunately, if the numbers had been adjusted for survivorship bias, the median manager performance statistics noted in table 4 would have been even *lower*. Survivorship bias occurs when failed mutual funds are excluded from the median manager performance statistics because those failed funds no longer exist. Not including the "loser funds" skews the median manager averages higher. If these "loser funds" (which, no doubt, had poor performance or else they would have remained in existence) were added back into the calculated averages, the per-

Table 4: Actively-Managed Canadian Mutual Funds vs. Index and Exchange-Traded Fund Returns (as of 31 December 2012)

	1 yr	5yr	10 yr
SHORT-TERM CANADIAN BONDS			
Median Mutual Fund Manager in Short Term Cdn. Bonds	1.30%	3.00%	2.80%
DEX Short Term Bond Index	2.01%	4.64%	4.38%
iShares DEX Short Term Bond Index Fund (XSB)	1.72%	4.33%	4.34%
Index-based ETF advantage over median manager	0.42%	1.33%	1.54%
CANADIAN BONDS			
Median Mutual Fund Manager in Cdn. Bonds	3.00%	4.90%	4.20%
DEX Universe Bond Index	3.60%	6.35%	5.97%
iShares DEX Universe Bond Index Fund (XBB)	3.26%	6.00%	5.73%
Index-based ETF advantage over median manager	0.26%	1.10%	1.53%
CANADIAN EQUITY			
Median Mutual Fund Manager in Cdn. Equity	6.60%	-1.30%	6.80%
S&P/TSX Capped Composite Index	7.19%	0.81%	9.21%
iShares S&P/TSX Capped Composite Index Fund (XIC)	6.89%	.58%	9.06%
Index-based ETF advantage over median manager	0.29%	1.88%	2.26%
U.S. EQUITY			
Median Mutual Fund Manager in U.S. Equity	10.10%	-1.30%	0.60%
S&P 500 Index (total return)	13.04%	1.64%	2.26%
iShares S&P 500 Index Fund (IVV)	12.82%	1.53%	2.22%
Index-based ETF advantage over median manager	2.72%	2.83%	1.62%
INTERNATIONAL EQUITY			
Median Mutual Fund Manager in International Equity	15.20%	-5.10%	2.00%
MSCI EAFE (net dividend)	14.32%	-3.71%	3.32%
iShares MSCI EAFE Index Fund	14.10%	-3.81%	3.21%
Index-based ETF advantage over median manager	-1.10%	-1.29%	1.21%
EMERGING MARKET EQUITY			
Median Mutual Fund Manager in Emerging Market Equity	13.60%	-3.00%	9.00%
MSCI Emerging Market Index (net dividend)	15.50%	-0.91%	11.26%
iShares MSCI EAFE Index Fund	14.19%	-1.15%	n/a
Index-based ETF advantage over median manager	0.59%	1.85%	n/a

Source: Globeandmail.com, Standard & Poor's Index Services Group, MSCI data © MSCI 2013, Scotia Capital Inc., Blackrock Inc.

formance gap between the active median manager and the index and exchange-traded funds would be even greater, thus favouring the index approach even more.

The Injustice of Survivorship Bias and Investor Frustration

Have you ever received a letter from an investment management company announcing that the fund in which you have invested will cease to exist or will be merged with another fund or manager at a certain date? If so, chances are that you were in an investment that had poor relative performance. Dealing with strategies that fail or cease to exist is a thorn in the side of investors. Not only is it a frustrating experience for the investor, but the lack of transparency in how the fund industry deals with its failed strategies is even more disturbing. In fact, failed funds and their performance statistics are wiped off of the industry statistics as if they never even existed. Does this seem right to you? Obviously not. But this is one of active management's dirtiest secrets. According to Standard & Poor's, 31% of Canadian equity funds, 36% of U.S. equity funds, and 29% of International equity funds in Canada failed over the five-year period ending 31 December 2011. In other words, during this period, one in three investment strategies did not make it and were simply liquidated or merged into another strategy.

Why Do Active Managers Underperform the Indexes?

As a group, active managers tend to underperform their benchmarks due to the combination of two factors.

1. The public capital markets are reasonably efficient and tend to price securities fairly well over long periods of time, leaving little room for "outsmarting."

How do the public capital markets become efficient? Primarily due to the tens of thousands of very smart, hard-working security analysts, investment managers, institutional pension funds, and investors who spend countless hours trying to find and buy incorrectly-priced securities. The active managers themselves and all the other securities experts make the public markets smart and fairly efficient.

Another way of looking at this is as follows: if an active manager out-performed the indexes because he or she was able to identify and buy mis-priced securities, it would mean that he or she somehow saw something that the tens of thousands of other analysts or managers did not. This may happen on occasion, but identifying an active manager who can outsmart the entire set of active managers across the dimensions of risk and return in the public markets—consistently over long periods of time—is like finding a needle in a haystack. As we will see in the next chapter, managers with 5-star ratings do not necessarily deliver a 5-star investment experience.

For these reasons, the data shows that there are simply not that many *imperfections* or *incorrectly-priced securities* left in the public markets for active managers to identify and buy. The fact that the markets are smart and fairly efficient over long periods of time is the ultimate compliment to active managers. Their collective contributions ensure that the market is efficiently priced.

2. The fees and total costs of active management act as a huge hurdle and leave little room for "outperformance."

Active management comes with a hefty price tag. In many consumer-oriented industries, a higher price is often linked to a higher-quality product and may represent better value over the long term. We know that premium products often last longer than lower-cost alternatives and there are many examples of products and services where it pays to spend a little more. Unfortunately, active investment management is not one of those industries—despite what the active managers would have you believe. The total cost associated with active management is extremely high and acts as an impediment for active managers to overcome. The total cost includes the following:

Figure 8: The Total Cost of Investing

- **MERs:** The most commonly known annual fee charged by investment counsellors, mutual funds, or portfolio WRAP programs to their investors. These fees can range from 0.5% to 3.0%, depending on the type of service and strategy offered. Typically, the MER consists of fees to cover a combination—but not necessarily all—of the following expenses: the selling agent, the servicing advisor, and the portfolio manager; TV, radio, and print advertising; all other promotional events; and accounting and record keeping.
- **Trading Commissions:** Possibly one of the largest additional expenses attached to active trading. Trading commissions are what the manager must pay to the brokerage industry for actively buying and selling investments inside the pool of capital being managed. Estimates for active management can range from 20 basis points to 75 basis points, depending on the amount of trading that occurs in the pool. Index-based asset class investments typically average between 1 and 5 basis points for their trade commissions.

- ◆ **Market Maker Spread:** The difference between the bidding and asking prices that the specialist sets for a stock. The specialist keeps the difference as compensation for providing liquidity. For less liquid stocks, the specialist has greater exposure to adverse price movements and likely will make the spread larger.
- ◆ **Market Impact Costs:** These costs reflect the change in the market price of a security due to a large block trade coming to the market.
- ◆ **Opportunity Costs:** The effective cost of security price movements that occur before the trade is actually executed.

Figure 8 illustrates the multiple layers of costs (both direct and indirect) associated with any pooled investment offering (mutual fund, investment counsellor, ETF, or institutional pool).

Advantages of Index-Based and Passively-Managed Asset Class Strategies

Prior to the last decade, individual Canadian investors needed active managers to expose us to a variety of different asset classes. We had no choice but to accept all the costs associated with gaining admission to those investment opportunities. Fortunately, times have changed and the options open to Canadian investors have become far more attractive. The benefits of index-based ETFs or passively-managed factor-based asset class funds from Dimensional Fund Advisors include diversification, consistency, transparency, lower costs and fees, competitive performance, tax efficiency, and simplicity.

Diversification
A diversified portfolio is essential for an investment plan to be successful. Indexing is an ideal way to diversify your portfolio. Actively-managed funds cannot compete with the diversification achieved by index funds relative to a market segment. This is due to the fact that index funds tend to hold a majority of their securities in their target indexes.

Purity and Consistency

Asset class purity and consistency are very important for investors who want to be in control of their asset allocation. Investors can more easily achieve purity and consistency in indexed and passive strategies because they lack the manager drift risks and other challenges associated with active strategies. These strategies also help investors reduce the survivorship risks associated with active management strategies.

Transparency

Indexed and passive strategies aim to provide high transparency with respect to your investment holdings and investment philosophy. Active management strategies are often unclear and can yield surprising results that do not meet an investor's expectations.

Low Costs

Among the greatest benefits of index-based and passively-managed asset class funds are the low costs associated with running them. There are two significant reasons why this is the case:

- lower management expense ratios because index/passive funds don't require a large team to run them;
- lower transaction costs since index/passive funds typically perform fewer transactions than actively-managed funds because index managers use a buy-and-hold (as opposed to market-timing) approach.

Competitive Performance

Thanks to their emphasis on diversification and remarkably low costs, index-based and passively-managed asset class funds are designed to achieve very competitive returns over long periods of time.

Potential for Tax Efficiency

Tax efficiency in portfolio management has nothing to do with the federal or provincial taxes that you pay on your employment or business earnings. Instead, it involves trying to reduce and defer the taxes payable on the distributions you receive from your taxable investment portfolio (interest, dividends, and capital gains).

In managing equity portfolios for taxable investment accounts, your goal (aside from the risk and return goals) should be to minimize and manage any taxable capital gain distributions. By reducing your distributions, you create a deferred capital gain in your portfolio. The simple act of delaying the payment of your taxes produces something quite subtle but very powerful.

Over a long period, investors can enjoy compound returns on their deferred taxes and, of course, keep their share of the gains on those taxes. Added up, all these tiny pieces can represent 0.5% to 1.0% of additional returns over the long term (ten years and more). Not only are these additional returns real, they also represent a higher portion of the total returns in a low-return environment—which makes it that much more important to take advantage of tax-efficient strategies.

Due to their buy-and-hold approach and consequently fewer trades, index-based and passively-managed asset class funds usually realize and distribute less in capital gains. Studies dating back to 1993 have shown that taxes have a hugely negative impact on relative returns and that lower-turnover (stock trading) index strategies are a much more tax-efficient investment option than actively-traded mutual funds or investment counsellor strategies.[1]

Ease, Simplicity, and Elegance
Index-based and passively-managed asset class funds are precisely designed to accomplish a specific objective: to track the performance of a specific index or asset class. Investors appreciate the fact that with index funds, they always know how their money is being invested.

Index-based and passively-managed asset class investment strategies work in up markets, down markets, and sideways markets. Like the tortoise, these asset class investments make their gains at a slow and steady rate, easily out-pacing sexier strategies where it matters most—in your investment returns.

7

Stop Chasing Performance

THE SLIPPERY SLOPE OF MANAGER SELECTION

As we learned in chapter 6, active managers on average underperform their respective benchmarks over long periods. Yet there are still stories of marquee managers who are lauded in the press or in the industry as "ones to watch." Because of the attention shown these outperformers, investors remain skeptical that indexed or passive management is in fact the best solution.

Why do the rumours of star money managers persist? And why do individual investors believe that financial firms can identify superior managerial skill when hiring and promoting managers?

The answers lie in human nature. We want to believe that so-called positive financial outliers exist. We want to believe that their superior performance can be identified or predicted in advance. We all dream of participating in their successes and, of course, we hope that we can replicate their results. After all, super-achievers and superstars can be found in most commercial industries and sports. We rejoice in their exploits and celebrate them in popular culture. On the more mundane side, many of us witness employees or managers who work harder and achieve superior results. Why would this not be the case in money management?

You might think it would be easy to identify the next Wayne Gretzky or Michael Jordan of money management. You've probably been told that the selection methodologies used by large financial services firms are capable of consistently identifying future stars. After all, they advertise it as their specialty. Unfortunately, the evidence shows that the process of selecting money managers is spotty at best. The inability of financial firms to accurately and consistently predict future star managers is not due to a lack of effort: the randomness of short-term asset prices and the swings in underlying asset classes make it impossible to predict which managers will outperform their benchmarks.

Just when you think you or your financial firm has identified a superb manager with a great track record, the actual results from that point on often tend to disappoint. Why does this happen? Chances are that the asset class or manager style has already peaked. Many investors purchase or switch into a new investment strategy on the basis of strong "recent" performance. Unbeknown to them, they are buying investment management strategies at their peak and may very well get burned once they go out of favour.

In 2013, Vanguard published a paper entitled "Vanguard's Principles for Investing Success" that included some very insightful research on manager ratings and subsequent cash flows to these managers. Figure 9 shows how investors move money in and out of various mutual funds (rated 1-star to 5-star, with 5 stars being the best rating). It shows clearly that investors have consistently poured money and savings into the top-rated fund managers. Instinctively, this would appear to be the smart thing for investors to do. We make purchase decisions on many consumer products based on consumer or research reports; why wouldn't we do something similar when we search for money managers?

Over the years, research has shown that past manager performance is no guarantee of future success. It may seem counterintuitive not to take past performance into account, but it is absolutely necessary when deciding with whom to invest. Ironically, as figure 10 demonstrates, the highest-rated funds underperformed relative to their benchmark soon after being given their top ratings. The investment industry actively markets performance when selling its products. Investors are unfortunately all too willing to buy into this devil's dance.

Furthermore, how do you identify a potential star manager when they all look identical and their commentaries, outlooks, and marketing

Figure 9: Cash Flows to Star Managers (1992 to 2012)

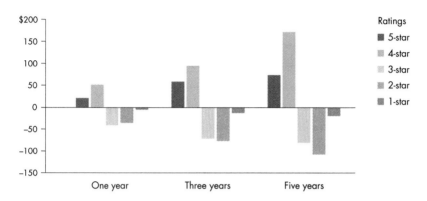

Cash flows for Morningstar-rated funds in periods after the ratings were posted.

Source: 2013 Vanguard white paper entitled "Vanguard's Principles for Investing Success."[1]

Figure 10: Star Manager Performance Relative to Benchmark

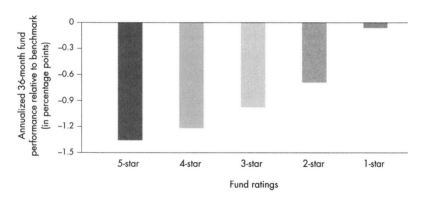

36-month annualized manager performance following a Morningstar rating.

Source: 2013 Vanguard white paper entitled "Vanguard's Principles for Investing Success."

statements all preach the same message. They all insist that their group/ manager is better and smarter than the rest. Investors are manipulated into believing that investing with them will yield better results than investing with their peers. Unfortunately, the evidence presents a much different story than their sales pitches would lead you to believe.

If you think that the manager selection challenge noted above is limited to retail investors using mutual funds, think again. Even at the most sophisticated levels of investing—the arena of the institutional pension fund—the manager selection process is unpredictable and lacks consistency. High-priced institutional consultants and high-level boards spend a tremendous amount of money and energy trying to make smart decisions around the hiring and firing of active managers. But research demonstrates that this practice fails to add value. In their 2008 paper "The Selection and Termination of Investment Management Firms by Sponsors" published in the *Journal of Finance*, Amit Goyal and Sunil Wahal shed some light on this complex decision-making process. They examined the actual selection and termination decisions between 1994 and 2003 of 3,400 institutional pension funds in the most cutthroat market—the U.S. institutional marketplace. Goyal and Wahal concluded that institutional plan sponsors typically "hire investment managers after large positive excess returns but that this return-chasing behaviour does not deliver positive excess returns thereafter." They determined that plan sponsors would have done just as well by leaving the fired manager in place instead of bringing in the high-performing new manager. What does this tell us about trying to hire and fire investment managers? If North America's top institutional pension manager selection experts themselves can't successfully predict and identify the next top manager, what hope do individual investors, their advisors, or their advisor firms have?

Searching for Stars Leads to Dangerous Behaviours

Trying to identify star managers leads investors astray and encourages them to chase performance or asset classes. Instead of buying low and selling high, investors tend to buy high and sell low.

Identifying star managers is even trickier for Canadian investors than it is for their American counterparts. Heavily influenced by U.S. investment news and trends, Canadian investors are also subject to trends from our resource-based and cyclical Canadian equity markets, exposing us to an extremely unsettling roller-coaster of star-manager marketing that includes investment themes and sector volatility.

Over the last twenty years, Canadian investors have had to live through many different investment swings and trends: the early 1990s included star Canadian junior resources and mining managers; U.S. consumer brand companies boomed during the mid-1990s; and the late 1990s heralded a new era for managers investing in global Internet and technology companies. The year 2000 saw an explosive marketing of managers in sectors such as global pharmaceuticals, finance, and technology, while real estate trust managers came to life in 2002 and income trusts by 2004. In 2007, Canadian investors were back to where they started with Canadian oil and gas and resource managers capturing a huge spotlight. Now, in 2013, investors are seeing U.S. stocks at an all-time high, with Canadian oil and gas stocks back in the doldrums. Canadian investors who tried to chase returns through these waves are likely to have drowned along the way.

Herein lies the main problem. Although investors may not realize it, searching for star managers is the same as chasing asset classes. Instead, investors should more closely examine performance attribution, comparisons to appropriate benchmarks, and risk factors. Informed and empowered investors must not mistake asset class factor performance for star manager performance.

Is There a Better Alternative to Searching for the Stars?

If the bad news is that identifying the stars is neither easy nor predictable, the good news is that we have a framework for portfolio construction that can help us create a long-term asset management blueprint. We also have investment tools such as asset class investments in the form of exchange-traded funds or Dimensional Fund Advisor's asset class funds that provide viable alternatives to traditional actively-managed offerings. These investment tools offer Canadian investors access to Canadian, U.S., and international equity markets and various risk factors (to be explained in the next chapter) in a precise fashion. Such investment tools capture the returns of the asset class in a much more transparent, tax-efficient, scientific, and cost-effective manner—and do so with less manager drift and selection risk.

8

Realize That Risk and Return Are Related

FACTOR-BASED INVESTING AND THE
FAMA/FRENCH THREE-FACTOR MODEL

You've become aware of the benefits of asset class investing, portfolio diversification theory, and index-based and passively-managed investments. But how should you go about implementing these concepts into your portfolio? What asset classes should you include? And in what proportion? Once again, academic research has shed light on these difficult yet important questions.

In June 1992, Eugene Fama of the University of Chicago Booth School of Business and Kenneth French of Dartmouth College published their landmark study, "The Cross Section of Expected Stock Returns" in the *Journal of Finance*. By identifying market, size, and value in returns, Fama and French developed a three-factor model for gauging returns relative to risk.

Their analysis of the sources of investment risk and return has reshaped portfolio management, greatly improving our understanding of the factors that drive performance and revolutionizing the way we construct asset class portfolios. The Fama/French three-factor model is a valuable tool for asset allocation and portfolio analysis.

Three Risk Factors Drive Returns

Fama and French studied historical stock market returns dating back to 1927. Their research improved upon what was then known in the investment world as the single-factor pricing model (CAPM) by identifying three factors to explain what drives the variation in portfolio returns. The three factors are:

- **Market Factor:** stocks have higher expected returns than bonds. This additional return reflects the "premium" demanded by investors for participating in a broadly-diversified portfolio of equities vs. the security of investing in fixed-income bonds.
- **Company Stock Price Factor:** low-priced "value" stocks have higher expected returns than high-priced "growth" stocks. This additional return reflects the "premium" demanded by investors for investing in relatively low-price (value) companies vs. relatively high-price (growth) companies.
- **Company Size Factor:** small company (small cap) stocks have higher expected returns than large company (large cap) stocks. This additional return reflects the "premium" demanded by investors for investing in small company stocks relative to large company stocks.

Fama and French's conclusion that stocks are riskier than bonds and therefore carry a greater possibility of returns was hardly breaking news. However, their discovery that small companies outperform large companies in returns and that value stocks far outstrip their more established cousins in growth markets was not common knowledge at the time. When applied to historical data, the Fama/French three-factor model can explain upwards of 96% of average equity performance.

The three-factor model shows investors and advisors where returns come from and illustrates the various expected returns from different asset classes better than any other deciding factors (e.g., market predictions, investment TV shows, manager strategies, newsletters, or the latest trendy ideas). To construct an investment portfolio that is right for you, you must decide to what extent your portfolio will be exposed to each of the three risk factors—market, size, and company value. The

Figure 11: Additional Returns for Each Factor in the Three-Factor Asset Pricing Model

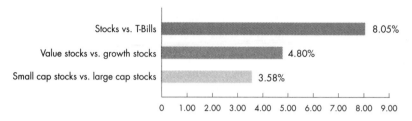

Source: Average annual returns from 1927 to 2012, U.S. market, data courtesy of Fama/French

greater your exposure to risk, the greater the expected return. Always remember that:

+ Investors cannot earn higher returns without taking on greater risk.
+ Total portfolio risk and return are the most important factors in constructing an investment plan.

Figure 11 compares the returns generated by each of these three factors. Although the given risk factor premiums are for the U.S. market from 1927 to 2012, we will demonstrate that these same factors are at play around the world.

Cost of Capital: Explaining the Risk/Return Relationship

A company's cost of capital is the financial explanation we use to better understand the results and implications of the three-factor equity model. Put simply, the cost of capital is the borrowing rate or discount rate that companies must pay to lenders or shareholders for access to their capital. From the investor's perspective, it is the expected return on their investment—the return needed to satisfy investors for the risk they are taking in the loan or equity purchase they make when investing in a company.

Small companies are riskier investments than larger companies and thus have a higher cost of capital. This is the case when they borrow funds from the bank and when they issue stock. Small companies should (and do, over the long term) provide greater rates of return for investors than larger companies. Investors will expect higher returns from small companies and price them accordingly into their lending rates or their expected stock return rates.

Similarly, "out of favour" (or value) companies are riskier than growth companies and have a higher cost of capital as a result. Investing in value companies should (and does, over the long term) provide greater rates of return for investors than growth companies. As with small companies, investors will expect higher returns to justify the risks of investing in companies that are out of favour.

How do "Factors" and "Premiums" Exist in an Efficient Market?

As strong supporters of the Efficient Market Hypothesis, Fama and French believe that the market is reasonably efficient and that, over-all, the market calculates security prices remarkably well over the long run. Therefore, they warn that it is very difficult to beat the market. However, they have identified two classes of stocks (the small company and value company stocks discussed above) that have higher expected returns relative to other segments of the market over long periods of time. How can this be? Fama and French concluded that the markets work quite well and are in fact simply pricing these riskier securities with higher expected risk premiums. Over the long term, investing in riskier companies should provide an additional return or premium relative to investing in safer companies. If that were not the case, then no one would invest in riskier companies in the first place.

The more you let the concept of value and small company investing sink in, the more these premiums and factors make sense. Consider this: you have the choice of investing in one of two companies. One is a safe, large company; the other, a large, well-known company that has fallen "out of favour" with investors due to various events. Which one would you invest in? If you were open to taking the risk of investing in the "out of favour" company, surely you would want a higher rate of return? Your suggested buying price would be reflected in your demand for a premium. This is exactly the type of evaluation process that occurs millions of times a day in equity markets around the world. With this in mind, understanding how these premiums exist becomes not only clearer but should also add to your confidence in why such premiums are a key component in becoming an empowered investor.

Improve Your Portfolio: Think Value Factor

What is value investing? Value investing—also known as contrarian investing or bargain hunting—is the investment approach that looks for stocks that are out of favour, neglected, forgotten, distressed, or beaten down. Such stocks are customarily called "value" stocks; their opposites are called "growth" stocks. Fama and French's research has confirmed what many market participants have been stating for years: "value" stocks outperform not only the broad market, but growth stocks as well.

A company's stocks can become value stocks for a variety of reasons: an overall decline in the industry sector; a challenging situation; a fall from favour. When such situations occur, a company's stock price may decrease even though its underlying book value remains unchanged. Both modest and significant changes in an industry can create anxiety about the future and generate opportunities for investors to pick up investments with higher expected returns.

As table 5 shows, the value effect exists in all major global markets. Over long periods of time, value stocks have demonstrated higher returns than those of broad market or growth stocks.

Savvy investors worldwide recognize that value investing is a better way to invest for the long term. The strategy is under-utilized, however, because of investment hype, performance chasing, and the short-term focus to which many investors succumb in their investment thinking.

Investors have a marked tendency to drift towards "growth stocks." Often these growth companies have high profiles, a glamorous image, and plenty of positive press in the media. But do these high-profile

Table 5: Value Stocks Outperform over the Long Term

Annualized compound returns (%)

Canadian Value Companies
11.64%

Canadian Companies (S&P/TSX Composite Index)
10.72%

Canadian Large Companies
7.50%

Study Period
1977–2012

U.S. Large Value Companies
11.69%

U.S. Companies (S&P 500 Index)
9.82%

U.S. Large Growth Companies
9.25%

Study Period
1927–2012

U.S. Small Value Companies
14.77%

U.S. Small Companies (CRSP 6-10)
11.54%

U.S. Small Growth Companies
8.69%

Study Period
1927–2012

International Large Value Companies
14.85%

International Companies (MSCI World ex U.S.)
10.69%

International Large Growth Companies
8.79%

Study Period
1975–2012

Emerging Market Large Value Companies
15.95%

Emerging Market Large Companies
12.27%

Emerging Market Large Growth Companies
10.25%

Study Period
1989–2012

Source: Dimensional Fund Advisors and E. Fama/K. French. All returns in USD except Canadian Market Stocks. Canadian Market stocks in CAD returns. Period of Study: Canadian Companies 1977–2012, U.S. Large Companies 1927–2012, U.S. Small Companies 1927–2012, International Companies 1975–2012, Emerging Market Companies 1989–2012.

Figure 12: The Underdog Wins

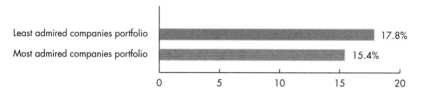

Stocks of firms with lower scores on the "Most Admired" list bested those ranked highest. Compound stock returns from 1983 to 2006,

Source: Anginer, Fisher, and Statman, chart, *Fortune*, 5 March 2007

companies make for good investments? Will they produce higher expected returns on a go-forward basis? Research has shown that they are not necessarily bad investments; rather, they are investments with *lower expected returns.*

Companies with the Best Reputations Do Not Always Have the Best-Performing Stocks

In a fascinating 2007 study, researchers compared the stock returns of the companies with the highest rankings on *Fortune Magazine*'s "Most Admired Companies" list to the returns of the companies with the lowest rankings on the same list. After reviewing stock returns over a twenty-three-year period from 1983 to 2006, researchers found that the stocks of firms with the lowest rankings actually did better than the stocks of firms with the highest rankings (see figure 12).

The Underdog Often Provides Better Returns

In addition to weaker reputations, the least admired companies had two distinguishing features. First, the companies at the bottom of the list had lower valuations such as stock market price to book value ratio over the study period. The average price-to-book ratio of the most admired companies was 2.07 compared with 1.27 for the least admired group. Second, the least admired companies tended to be smaller than the most admired companies and—as we discussed earlier in this chapter—investors can often obtain higher returns by investing in small, out-of-favour companies than in larger, higher-priced ones.

Patience Is Required to Capture the Value Premium

If investors are going to add and overweight the value factor in their diversified portfolios, they must recognize and understand the variability and short-term unpredictability of this factor. While investing in value companies would be much easier if there were a steady, consistent, and regularly-added premium given to investors, it is unfortunately not the case.

Investing in value companies is still adding risk to portfolios and this will show up differently over various economic cycles. Figure 13 shows the long-term average U.S. value premium from 1927 to 2012 (dashed horizontal line). Other global markets have very similar value patterns, but we have used the U.S. value premium in this example because it is the market with the longest track record. Note the large annual variations (of value stocks minus growth stocks) that have occurred over this eighty-year period. There is good reason for investors to be extremely patient in order to capture the value premium.

Executing Your Value Investing Strategy

Any diversified portfolio can include the value effect in its Canadian, U.S., International, or Emerging Market stock components. When adding value to your portfolio, remember these key execution strategies:

- ◆ Capture your value effect by investing in a diversified basket of high book-to-market ratio securities ("value stocks") rather than choosing a few distressed securities through "stock picking."
- ◆ As with any other investment style, value stocks go in and out of favour and require an investment strategy with long-term discipline (ten years and beyond).

Figure 13: U.S. Value Premium 1927 to 2012

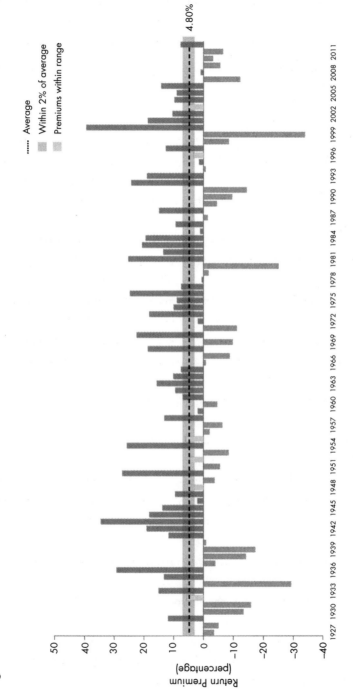

Yearly observations: value stocks minus growth stocks

Source: Multi-factor data provided by Fama/French.[1]

- Use index-based or passively-managed factor-based transparent portfolio management tools (discussed in chapter 5) that offer pure exposure to the value factor, thereby increasing your control over your total investment strategy.

Improve Your Portfolio: Think Small Factor

The last decade has provided dramatic evidence of the benefits of diversifying your portfolio by including small capitalization stocks. A portfolio that included an allocation of diversified small companies in Canadian, U.S., International, and Emerging Markets would have weathered the storms of the past decade much better than a portfolio entirely allocated to large companies (see figure 14).

Rolf Banz of the University of Chicago Booth School of Business was the first to identify the small company effect. In 1981, he published a report based on his analysis of NYSE companies from 1926 to 1975, and concluded that, in the long term, small companies behave differently than larger companies and have higher expected returns.

Table 6 shows that, as with value stocks, the small company effect exists worldwide. This is apparent from their higher returns relative to their larger rivals. As a group, Canadian small value companies outperformed Canadian broad market companies, as did U.S. and international small company stocks relative to U.S. and international large company stocks. Interestingly enough, when compared to other segments in the same marketplace, the market segment with the highest returns was made up of small-value companies. This is precisely what Eugene Fama and Ken French's research told us to expect: small and out-of-favour companies carry the highest level of risk, and should therefore have the highest expected rates of return.

Steer Clear of Small-Growth Companies

Ironically, investing in small-growth companies offers few benefits for portfolio management. All over the world, investors do not appear to have been compensated for the additional risks they take on when they

Figure 14: Growth of Wealth From January 2000 to December 2012

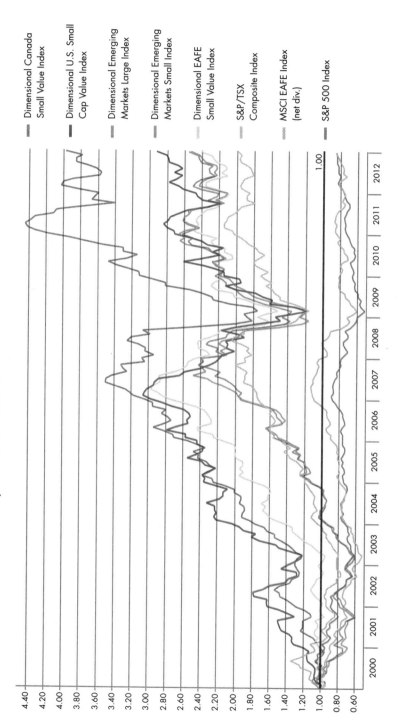

Legend:
- Dimensional Canada Small Value Index
- Dimensional U.S. Small Cap Value Index
- Dimensional Emerging Markets Large Index
- Dimensional Emerging Markets Small Index
- Dimensional EAFE Small Value Index
- S&P/TSX Composite Index
- MSCI EAFE Index (net div.)
- S&P 500 Index

Source: The S&P data are provided by Standard & Poor's Index Services Group. MSCI data copyright MSCI 2013, all rights reserved. S&P/TSX data provided by S&P/TSX. Dimensional Index data compiled by Dimensional.[2]

Table 6: Small Value Company Stocks Outperform over the Long Term

Annualized Compound Returns (%)

Canadian Small Value Companies	10.94%	
Canadian Small Companies	8.11%	Study Period 1994–2012
Canadian Companies (S&P/TSX Composite Index)	8.03%	
U.S. Small Value Companies	14.69%	
U.S. Small Companies (CRSP 6-10)	12.10%	Study Period 1951–2012
U.S. Companies (S&P 500 Index)	10.53%	
International Small Value Companies	13.25%	
International Small Companies	10.81%	Study Period 1981–2012
International Companies (MSCI World ex USA)	8.26%	

Source: Dimensional Fund Advisors and E. Fama/K. French. All returns in USD except Canadian Market Stocks. Canadian Market stocks in CAD returns. Period of Study: Canadian Companies 1994–2012, U.S. Companies 1951–2012, International Companies 1981–2012

invest in small-growth companies. In fact, many investors incorrectly invest in small-growth companies (either by buying stock in individual companies or buying mutual funds that invest in small companies with very high P/Es) with the expectation of seeing spectacular returns. Unbeknown to them, they are buying an asset class that has historically generated disappointing returns despite the elevated risk. If you want to increase your expected returns and are prepared to accept higher levels of volatility, you should look to invest in either small-value or small-blend company stocks and avoid investing in small-growth company stocks.

Investing in small companies is adding risk to portfolios that will show up differently over various economic cycles. Figure 15 shows the long-term average U.S. small company premium (dashed horizontal

Figure 15: U.S. Small Company Premium 1927 to 2012

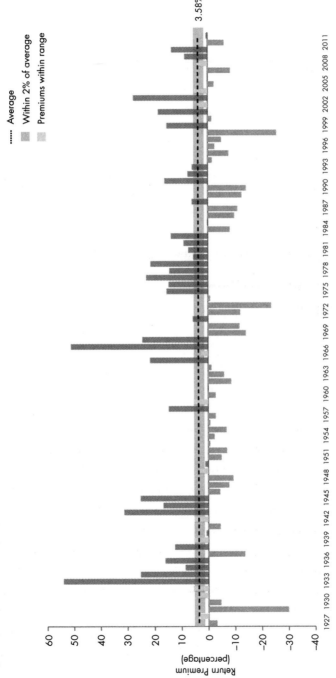

Legend:
- ······ Average
- Within 2% of average
- Premiums within range

3.58%

Return Premium (percentage)

Yearly observations: small stocks minus large stocks

Source: Multi-factor data provided by Fama/French.

line). Note the large annual variations (of small stocks minus large stocks) that have occurred over this eighty-year period. Other global markets will have very similar small company patterns. In order to successfully capture the small cap premium, investors must be patient and stay committed to their long-term investment allocations.

Executing Your Small Company Strategy

Any diversified portfolio can incorporate the small company effect in its Canadian, U.S., or International stock components. As with value stocks, keep these key execution strategies in mind when adding small companies to your portfolio:

- To capture the small company effect, invest in a diversified basket of small-value or small-core stocks. Do not choose a few small company securities through "stock picking."
- Like any other investment style, small company stocks go in and out of favour, sometimes for very long periods. They require an investment strategy with long-term discipline (ten years or longer).
- Use index-based or passively-managed factor-based transparent portfolio management tools (see chapter 5) that will provide pure exposure to small companies, thereby increasing your control over your total investment strategy.

As a final note on these risk factors, it is important to remember that the additional returns from investing in value and small company stocks are not guaranteed to materialize in your portfolio on an annual or even short-to-medium-term basis. Investors who invest in small and value companies must sometimes endure long, difficult periods of under-performance relative to general equity returns. Before investing in small and value company asset classes, investors should review their investment objectives, time horizons, tax considerations, and tolerance for risk and uncertainty.

Patience, a view towards long-term asset allocation, and the belief in this investment philosophy are essential if you are to benefit from the inclusion of these factors and asset classes in your portfolio.

Bringing It All Together

The winning investment principles discussed in chapters 3 through 8 are the key components to generating more stability and greater returns in your portfolio. Together they bring structure, knowledge, and discipline, while providing the necessary foundation that will tilt the odds dramatically in your favour and allow you to become the empowered investor you have always wanted to be.

9

Discover the Profitability Factor

THE NEW FRONTIER

The previous chapter detailed the impact and effects of Fama and French's 1992 study and the three-factor stock-pricing model that it created. Fama and French forever changed the way investors thought about expected stock returns and portfolio construction. Over the past two decades, a swath of research, data, and other evidence has supported Fama and French's research and findings and helped solidify our understanding of the factors that drive portfolio returns.

It is important to understand that, in order to be considered a dimension of expected stock returns, a factor or premium must meet certain criteria. Research must prove that a factor or premium is:

1 Sensible;
2 Persistent across time periods;
3 Pervasive across markets;
4 Robust to alternative specifications; and
5 Cost effective to capture in well-diversified portfolios.[1]

In the last six or seven years, academics including Fama and French have improved their ability to document and study how profitability affects a company's expected stock returns. In 2012, Robert Novy-Marx, a professor at the University of Rochester's Simon Graduate School of Business, published his research paper, *The Other Side of Value: The Gross Profitability Premium*. His research shows that, when predicting expected returns, a company's gross profitability has roughly the same weighting as—and is complementary to—its book-to-market value. Combining this finding with those of other studies has led to a major breakthrough in financial research on the profitability factor. The two most important findings of the recent research are:

- A company's current gross profitability (defined as earnings before interest, taxes, depreciation/book value—researchers have variations of this ratio) is a statistically significant proxy for the future profitability of the company.
- Holding the other factors constant, companies with higher gross profitability have higher returns than companies with lower gross profitability.

Some investors might wonder what all the fuss is about. Haven't we always known profitability was important? Is the idea that a company's increased profitability will lend itself to higher share prices that much of a stretch? What's the big deal?

All fair questions. Investors and stock-picking money managers have been speaking of profitability for decades. However, active management has unfortunately had difficulty realizing the potential of the profitability factor. Why? Some observers feel that the main challenge of active managers has been their inability to accurately "predict" future cash flows and profitability.

The real breakthrough in Novy-Marx's research is the discovery of a statistically reliable proxy for future profitability. Up until now, investors and asset managers did not have a consistent measure to use when implementing profitability into a portfolio process. The proxy was the "missing link".

The research of Novy-Marx, Fama and French, and others has proven that a profitability proxy exists that is statistically significant and reliable. This, in turn, made it possible for researchers to study returns. They were able to rank all companies in stock markets around the world by a company's profitability/book value. Novy-Marx's research demonstrates that, when all other factors are kept constant, stocks with higher

Table 7: Summary Statistic for the Direct Profitability Premium

Annualized Average Returns (%)

Canadian High Direct Profitability/Book	13.15%	
Canadian Low Direct Profitability/Book	4.48%	Study Period 1991–2012
Canadian High – Low (Profitability Premium)	8.67%	
U.S. High Direct Profitability/Book	16.69%	
U.S. Low Direct Profitability/Book	9.84%	Study Period 1975–2012
U.S. High – Low (Profitability Premium)	6.84%	
International High Direct Profitability/Book	8.93%	
International Low Direct Profitability/Book	2.81%	Study Period 1992–2012
International High – Low (Profitability Premium)	6.12%	
Emerging Market High Direct Profitability/Book	11.15%	
Emerging Market Low Direct Profitability/Book	4.31%	Study Period 1996–2012
Emerging Market High – Low (Profitability Premium)	6.84%	

Source: Dimensional Fund Advisors using CRSP, Compustat, and Bloomberg data.[2]

gross profitability have higher returns than stocks with low profitability, thus generating a profitability premium. Researchers at Dimensional have come up with their own profitability measure called direct profitability. Direct profitability is equal to sales, less the cost of goods sold, less the cost of selling, general, and administrative expenses, less interest scaled by book value. Table 7 shows that a sizable profitability premium exists in most major markets including the Canadian, U.S.,

International, and Emerging Markets. Returns were controlled for size and relative price effects.

Novy-Marx's research discovered that the profitability premium has several interesting aspects. Firstly, profitability proved just as useful as book-to-market value when it came to forecasting returns. Secondly, including the profitability factor in the process of constructing a portfolio provided some significant diversification benefits, especially in a portfolio of value stocks. It turns out that the profitability factor and the value factor have low correlations to each other, making them ideal components to be co-mingled into a portfolio process.

Risk and Return Are Still Related

As explained in chapter 8, the relationship between risk and return was discovered by researchers who believe that the stock market is efficient and stock prices are fair and incorporate all available information. Therefore, investors demand higher expected returns when taking on more risk in their investments. To show how this relates to profitability, we can compare two companies, A and B, with identical direct profitability (see chart 1). However, because Company A is trading at a lower relative price compared to Company B, this means that Company A has a higher cost of capital. Company A has a lower relative price because investors perceive a greater risk in the company and will therefore demand a lower stock price and a higher expected return. This is the value premium that we explained earlier in chapter 8.

In chart 2, companies C and D have the same relative share price but because Company C has higher direct profitability, it will have higher expected returns. The more profitable Company C has the same relative price as the less profitable Company D for a reason—investing in Company C is perceived as riskier and therefore the company has a higher cost of capital.

Academic debate over the exact cause of the expected profitability premium is ongoing. While proponents of efficient markets embrace the theory of risk and return, other market researchers believe that the profitability premium may be the result of the mispricing of securities.

Chart 1

Large Cap Company	Relative Price (P/B)	Direct Profitability	Higher Expected Return
Company A	3.33	0.43	✓
Company B	6.09	0.43	

Chart 2

Large Cap Company	Relative Price (P/B)	Direct Profitability	Higher Expected Return
Company C	3.76	0.68	✓
Company D	3.74	0.29	

Source: Charts 1 and 2 courtesy of Dimensional Fund Advisors

However, regardless of the original cause, the fact remains that the profitability premium exists.

Profitability Factor Going Forward

The discovery of the proxy has made it possible to integrate the profitability factor into factor-based, passively-managed asset class investment strategies. Leading edge asset managers such as Dimensional Fund Advisors and AQR Capital Management are beginning to incorporate profitability into their multi-factor portfolio solutions and ETF makers will likely adopt it soon as well.

The profitability factor will add to and complement the Fama/French three-factor model. Applied correctly in a well-diversified portfolio, the profitability premium will complement existing tilts to value and small company strategies. The profitability premium is the latest frontier in factor and evidence-based strategies and we will be monitoring its development closely.

10

Create an Investment Policy Statement

THE FIRST DAY OF THE REST OF YOUR LIFE

The previous chapters set the stage for the investment world you live in, and provided you with tools and strategies to navigate it. Now we're entering the final phase on the journey to becoming an empowered investor. It's time to take the theory that you've learned and put it into practice. As it is in life, so it is in investing—execution is everything. These next few chapters will prepare you for the task at hand once you finish this book. You've learned what needs to be done; now you just need to do it.

You wouldn't prepare to build a new home or renovate your existing one without first thinking through your vision, drawing up architectural plans, selecting the right contractors and tradespeople, and planning ahead for possible budget overruns and surprises. Yet many people approach their long-term investments without any plan at all. An investment policy statement (IPS) is a written document that you and your advisor create to keep you and your investments on track. The IPS brings clarity, vision, and discipline to the investment process. Think of it as a personal investment road map for long-term investment success.

Advisory Firm's Investment Philosophy Pledge

If you're building or managing investment wealth over the long term, you need to adopt a comprehensive investment philosophy that will guide you along the way. The IPS integrates your personal objectives and financial situation with your investment strategies and your investment philosophy. An IPS should spell out that philosophy and help you and your advisory firm put it into practice with the ongoing management of your investments. This also serves as a pledge by the advisory firm that determines how your portfolio will be managed. The following is an example of how an investment philosophy may be spelled out in your IPS using the principles of *The Empowered Investor.* The pledge below is from our firm's IPS.

Pledge 1: Consistent process for managing investments

We have an investment process which includes the following components: a thorough know-your-client process, an investment policy process, standardized and consistent portfolio practices, fairness of client allocation policies, regular rebalancing, regular current-vs.-target portfolio reviews, full investment transparency, and professional investment reporting.

Pledge 2: Diversified global approach to investing

We take a global approach within the equity component of each client portfolio to enhance diversification and provide participation in equity appreciation opportunities worldwide. Portfolios will typically include: Canadian, U.S., International, and Emerging Markets equity exposure (unless otherwise stated in your investment policy statement).

Pledge 3: The inclusion of value and small cap companies:

We will include exposure to **broad equity market, value companies** and **small cap companies** in each major geographic equity component in your portfolio: Canadian, U.S., and International and Emerging Markets. We include value and small cap exposure as a way to increase the expected long-term returns of your portfolio. Long-term periods and patience are required to fully capture the value and small cap premiums.

Pledge 4: Using asset class investments

We will execute your portfolio strategy using asset class investment vehicles. By using passively-managed asset class exposure we are able to provide our clients with full and consistent long-term exposure to **broad equity market, value companies, and small cap companies.** As an independent firm we are able to use the best investments possible to execute these strategies. We do not build portfolios through individual stock selection or through the selection of active money managers.

Pledge 5: Rebalancing your portfolio:

We will rebalance your portfolio on a regular basis to ensure that it is in line with your long-term IPS "target" allocation. Our primary method of rebalancing is through cash flow management (deposits and withdrawals). When investing your deposits, we will buy asset classes that are underweighted relative to your long-term IPS targets. When raising cash to fund your withdrawals, we will sell asset classes that are over-weighted relative to your long-term IPS targets. On occasion we might rebalance portfolios due to significant market readjustments. This rebalancing process helps us buy "low" and sell "high" for your investment accounts on a consistent basis over the life of your portfolio.

Pledge 6: No market timing

We will not engage in any form of market timing. We will not attempt to make any significant shift in weightings from stocks to bonds or vice versa based on economic forecasts or any "gut feeling." We will not attempt to shift assets based on forecasts of business cycles (expansions or contractions) as this is too unpredictable. Not only would it detract from your investment returns, it would also add unnecessary risk and stress to your investment experience. Regular rebalancing will occur within Investment Policy Guidelines.

Pledge 7: No speculation

We will not speculate with *any* portion of your investments.

An IPS Provides Discipline and Structure

An IPS provides you and your advisor with the discipline needed to overcome common behavioural pitfalls. In a 2011 paper, Andrew Ang and Knut Kjaer pointed out that long-term investors have several advantages over those with shorter horizons. These include being able to take advantage of rebalancing opportunities: in other words, buying assets when they have temporarily declined in price. However, this is emotionally difficult because periods of market turmoil tempt investors to abandon the rules. "The paradox is that it is precisely during such challenging times that you most need the rules," write Ang and Kjaer.[1]

Institutional investors have been using investment policy statements for decades. Ang and Kjaer report, for example, that the Norwegian sovereign wealth fund followed a stringent set of rules for rebalancing during the financial crisis of 2008–2009, buying equities while others sold in a panic. As a result, the fund enjoyed great success during the rebound that followed.

The IPS is no longer the sole domain of large pension plans; it is a key tool for individual investors too. In many ways, private investors have more to gain from developing an IPS because individuals have a much deeper emotional attachment to their money than do pension fund managers and can therefore greatly benefit from the discipline, structure, and process set out by the plan.

An IPS is Your Living Document

An IPS and a financial plan are not the same. The focus of an IPS is on the ongoing management of your long-term portfolio. A financial plan

Figure 16: Your Personal Details Bring Your IPS to Life

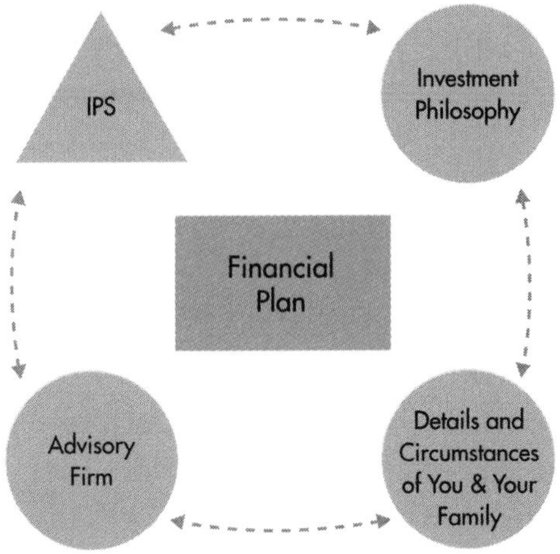

on the other hand, is more encompassing and will look into your entire financial affairs, including important items such as retirement planning, budgeting and savings, analysis of cash flow, risk management (insurance), and wills and estate management.

There are many different components that form an IPS. Developing each of these components will require careful thought and analysis.

Your investment goals: Are you investing for capital preservation, long-term growth, or a mix of both? Are you currently adding new money to your portfolio, or are you drawing on it for income?

Your expectations: Based on your proposed asset allocation and asset classes to be used, you should learn and become aware of how they might work over long periods of time. What have good periods looked like and what have poor periods looked like. You should be made aware of the impact of inflation and taxes on long-term investments.

Your time horizon: Are you investing for a child's education in ten years or a retirement that may last thirty years? As a general rule, the longer the time horizon, the more risk you can take in the portfolio.

Your understanding of risk: There are many types of risk for investors. IPS discussions should cover the following risks:

- *Volatility*: The magnitude of the losses and gains that all portfolios will experience over time. (In financial terms, volatility is the standard deviation of returns.) Markets do not move in a straight line and investors must understand how much downward movement they can tolerate, both financially and emotionally.
- *Financial risk*: The dollar or percentage amount of decline you can accept, given your need for capital preservation, income and your overall level of wealth.
- *Emotional risk*: The amount of decline you can accept without being tempted to abandon your strategy. This risk will vary based on your personality and previous experience with investments.
- *Purchasing power risk*: The risk that your investment returns will not keep pace with inflation over time. Over long-term periods, this risk is typically higher with bond and GIC investments.
- *Longevity risk*: The risk that an investor will outlive his or her portfolio. Implementing a sustainable annual draw-down is one way to help manage this risk.

Your asset classes: Which asset types (government bonds, corporate bonds, Canadian stocks, U.S. stocks, international stocks, etc.) will be included in your portfolio and which will be avoided? You should understand the characteristics of each of these asset classes, and how they have evolved over time.

Your asset allocation strategy: What will the portfolio's strategic asset mix be? (For example, will the portfolio set a target of 60% equities and 40% fixed income?)

Your tax situation: What tax-efficiency strategies will be used to minimize taxes in non-registered accounts?

Your investment costs: What are the costs associated (at all levels) with the investment strategies?

Monitor, evaluate, and report: How will the portfolio be rebalanced back to the target allocation? How often will you receive statements showing your holdings, account balances, and performance?

Embrace the IPS Process – It's Yours!

The process of creating and maintaining an IPS will ultimately empower you and your advisory firm to set the winning conditions for a better long-term investment outcome. The ongoing IPS dialogue with a trusted advisor will provide you with a better long-term investment experience by making you more aware of how markets work, allowing you to set realistic objectives and reduce the number of future surprises. The IPS also provides you with full transparency concerning the role of the advisory firm.

Your investment strategy should strike a balance between all the components mentioned above. You may choose to work with a qualified advisor to construct a customized IPS and then have the investment strategy executed, monitored, updated, and reported back to you. Or you may choose to create and monitor an IPS on your own. However you choose to create your IPS, recognize that it represents a crucial ingredient in investment success.

11

Take Control of Your Personal Financial Plan

COORDINATE YOUR INVESTMENTS
WITH YOUR LIFE PLAN

When I speak with clients and investors, most of the conversations revolve around investing. Managing your portfolio (which we do with an IPS) is a crucial part of our work, but it must be seen as part of the big picture. A personal financial plan is just as valuable to your long-term success.

While an IPS focuses exclusively on your investments, a personal financial plan is much broader. It focuses on you and your family, bringing all your financial and life goals together into one planning exercise. This includes saving for retirement, debt management, insurance, taxes, and estate planning. Part of becoming an empowered investor is being able to create a sustainable financial future for you and your family. Often, too much is focused on the portfolio while life-affecting financial concepts are neglected.

Do you know when you want to retire and do you know how much money you need to make it happen? Do you know how much you should be saving for your children's education or for your dream cottage? What planning strategies could help you save taxes? Do you have the proper risk management and safety nets in place? Most Canadians do not know the answers to these questions. For example, according to a poll conducted by ING Direct in 2012, more than two-thirds of Canadians have no financial plan for their retirement.

Unfortunately, retiring comfortably will be a challenge for many Canadians: in fact, many younger baby-boomers and the members of

Figure 17: Personal Savings as a Percentage of Personal Disposable (After-Tax) Income

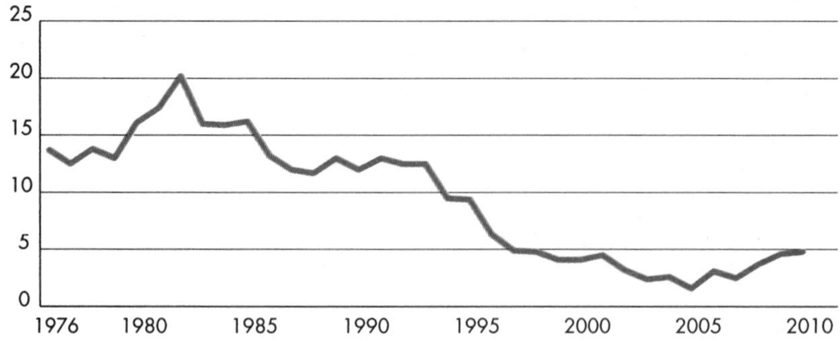

Source: Statistics Canada

Generation X (born between the mid-1960s and late 1970s) will experience a lower standard of living than their parents. Those who raised families during the late 1990s and 2000s often bore the weight of big mortgages and stagnating wages, and few have defined benefit pension plans at work. They also did not inherit the frugality of previous generations; savings rates today are extremely low (see figure 17), and many use lines of credit to live beyond their means. In the past, Canadians saved with discipline and diligence through some of the toughest financial periods. Empowered investors understand that they need to return to that philosophy.

For those who are serious about planning for the future, a comfortable retirement is still within reach. The important first step is to create a personal financial plan.

How to Know If You Need a Financial Plan

Most, if not all, Canadians need some type of financial plan or guide, often at multiple stages in their lives. The following questions can help you to decide whether you need professional help in putting your plan together:

- Do you know how much total investment wealth is required to finance your retirement?
- Do you know how much you should be saving on an annual basis to reach your retirement goals?
- Do you have the time to attend to your personal financial affairs?
- Are you confused about conflicting financial advice from several sources?
- Do you feel that you are paying too much tax?
- Do you feel that you can't make ends meet?
- Do you feel that you can't save any money?
- Has there been a recent change in your life that could affect your financial future, such as retirement, job loss, an inheritance, the sale or purchase of a business, an addition to your family, or the loss of your spouse?

The six-step financial planning process highlighted in figure 18 is a set of guidelines adopted by many financial planning associations around the world. It will help you and your family better understand how financial planning professionals can work with you to help you achieve your personal goals.

One Size Doesn't Fit All

The financial planning process is an important exercise in striving to control your personal and financial destiny. As the American politician Robert F. Bennett wrote: "Your life is the sum result of all the choices you make, both consciously and unconsciously. If you can control the process of choosing, you can take control of all aspects of your life. You can find the freedom that comes from being in charge of yourself."

Everyone has different goals and challenges, and no two family circumstances look alike. There are so many things in life that make us unique. We make important life decisions—to own a business or be an employee, to get married or remain single, to have children or not, to retire early or to continue to work as long as possible. When you

Figure 18: The Six-Step Financial Planning Process

Step 1	Establish the client-planner relationship by clarifying the responsibilities of the planner and the client.
Step 2	Identify your personal goals and objectives by collecting and assessing all relevant financial data—assets and liabilities, tax returns, investments, insurance policies, wills, and pension plans.
Step 3	Identify and analyse the personal data, including financial problems that can create barriers to your financial independence.
Step 4	Create a written plan with recommendations structured to meet your needs without undue emphasis on purchasing specific investment products.
Step 5	Implement your personal financial plan to ensure that you reach your goals and objectives.
Step 6	Schedule a periodic review and revision of your plan to ensure that you achieve your goals.

add life's many challenges (both pleasant and unpleasant) to the equation, you can see how financial planning can become a very personal life-planning exercise.

There are also many dimensions or phases within a personal financial plan that will depend on what life stage you are at (see figure 19 for financial planning phases). Individuals, couples, and families evolve through these dimensions and phases over time; their financial priorities will do so as well.

Putting It All Together

Your portfolio is just one part of an overall financial strategy. By integrating your investment strategy with your financial plan, you'll enjoy the confidence, comfort, and peace of mind that come from knowing

Figure 19: Financial Planning Phases

Accumulation Phase (ages 25–50)	Pre-Retirement Phase (ages 50–70)	Retirement Phase (ages 65–90)
• Saving 10 to 20% of family earnings • Debt elimination • Children's education • Protecting your family with insurance • Wills & POAs up-to-date • Investment focus: long-term growth	• Increase savings to 20% or more of family earnings • Debt elimination • Protecting your family with insurance • Wills & POAs up-to-date • Investment focus: moderate growth	• Determining a sustainable portfolio draw-down rate • Estate planning • Wills & POAs up-to-date • Leaving a legacy or not • Charitable giving • Investment focus: capital preservation with some growth

that your money is working for your interests. This will allow you to concentrate your energy and passion on the things that matter most: your family, your friends, your business or profession, your hobbies, and your retirement.

Conclusion: The Blue Ocean

BECOMING THE INVESTOR YOU ALWAYS WANTED TO BE

In 2005, W. Chan Kim and Renée Maubourgne wrote *The Blue Ocean Strategy*, a business management book that sought to change how companies competed. Their main argument was that a company needed to move from the "red ocean," where it is engaged in bloody and ruthless competition in a discouraging and dwindling marketplace, to the "blue ocean," where its strategies and offerings set it apart from its competition, creating a unique demand for its products and services. When companies create such a powerful, independent business environment, they are said to be operating in the blue ocean.

We've adopted and adapted Kim and Maubourgne's metaphor to the world of personal investing to describe two investing environments— the murky ocean and the blue ocean. By escaping the murky ocean, investors can reduce the stress of investing, gain peace of mind, and increase their chances of long-term investment success. The blue ocean is the ideal environment for you and your investments and the final destination of the empowered investor.

The Murky Ocean

The environment of the murky ocean is chaotic and confusing. Without an investment plan or philosophy to guide you, you're vulnerable to hype and market storms, and prone to anxiety and frustration. You may be unaware of the conflicts of interest at play in the financial services industry or unsure of how to navigate them. The sales forces from brokerage and mutual fund firms are constantly pitching new ideas, new strategies, and new products to you, encouraging you to follow active investment strategies that have you chasing performance, trading heavily, trying to time the market, and making big bets on predictions. As a result, your investments are disorganized, heavily concentrated in one industry, or minimally diversified. High fees and trading costs eat into the worth of your portfolio and returns are inconsistent—even though your advisors promise that they have the inside scoop on selecting the next star performers.

In the murky ocean, a lack of clarity and transparency makes it difficult to understand how your money is being managed or why your advisor is recommending one investment over another. Feeling as if the investment process is out of your control feeds your fear that you may not reach your personal investment goals in time for your retirement.

The murky ocean is the worst place an investor can be. But with better education and awareness, investors can steer their investments into the blue ocean.

The Blue Ocean

In the blue ocean, your financial well-being is the top priority. It's an environment that will help you avoid the shoals of conflicts of interest and the waves of market hype. And while it will not necessarily insulate you from market storms and the uncertainty of short-term price movements, understanding what you can and cannot control will help you weather those storms with much less stress and more chance of success.

The blue ocean is the clear, transparent environment you will discover by becoming an empowered investor and following the eight principles of successful investing we have discussed in this book. Those principles can be summarized as:

1. Steer clear of the most common investment pitfalls.
Being aware of common investment pitfalls is half the battle. Ignore "expert" market predictions and resist the urge to chase star perform-

ers. Control your emotions so that they do not have a negative impact on your investment results. Be aware of the mathematics of sustainability and calculate how much money you will require for a financially independent future. Then build a plan that will ensure that you reach this goal.

2. Recognize conflicts of interest in the financial services industry.

By understanding how the financial industry works, you will be able to take better care of your money. A qualified, independent, fee-based advisor does not depend on commissions or sales fees and is able to offer unbiased advice and recommend the best tools in the marketplace.

3. Choose asset class investing.

Asset class investing has been proven to have a bigger impact on your portfolio than market timing or stock picking. It is the most important step in taking control of your investments.

4. Build a diversified portfolio that is highly structured, organized, and follows a rebalancing process.

A truly well-diversified portfolio will include: bonds, real estate investment trusts, Canadian large cap, value, and small cap stocks, U.S. large cap, value, and small cap stocks, International value and small cap stocks, and Emerging Market stocks.

Most investors and many advisors misunderstand the concept of diversification, believing that they are diversified because they own fifteen stocks or ten mutual funds. Too much overlap equals improper diversification and can be a recipe for disaster.

Your portfolio should be rebalanced on a regular basis to ensure that it is in line with your long-term "target" allocations.

5. Choose passively-managed, index-based or factor-based asset class investments that are tax-efficient.

Passively-managed, index- or factor-based asset class investment tools have been shown to consistently outperform actively-managed funds. Choose tools that are transparent, precise, tax-efficient, and flexible.

6: Discover that risk and return are related. Consider including small and value companies when designing your portfolio.
Use the Fama/French Three-Factor model to create the optimal portfolio structure for long-term success. This model shows that:

* stocks outperform bonds
* value stocks outperform growth stocks
* small company stocks outperform large company stocks

7. Create an investment policy statement (IPS).
An IPS defines your investment goals, describes your investment philosophy, and determines how your portfolio will be managed. A qualified, fee-based investment advisor can help you create an IPS that will keep your investments on track and within your specified risk parameters, greatly enhancing your investment experience.

8. Coordinate your investments with your life plan.
Investments and life should work together; a well-considered plan is crucial to ensuring that your dreams become financially viable.

While we would all like to find ourselves and our investments in an environment like the blue ocean, simply wishing for it to happen won't make it come true. Success in investing—as in life itself—is the result of hard work, proper diligence, and the application of the best strategies. The eight principles of successful investing, while interesting and worthwhile in and of themselves, become most powerful when integrated into an overall financial strategy. Not only will you increase the odds that you will obtain better performance from your portfolio over the long term, but the side benefits are very real and very human. By taking control of the way you invest, you gain control of your future financial well-being. The methods in this book won't help you predict the future, but they will prepare you for it.

The last few years have been a trying time for investors worldwide. While we don't believe in speculating on future market movements, we are confident that the principles and strategies discussed in *The Empowered Investor* are the best guides on the uncertain road ahead. Their

Table 8: Comparative Summary of Murky and Blue Oceans

Aspects	Murky Ocean	Blue Ocean
Portfolio structure	• disorganized collection of funds • concentrated stock picks • diversified using multiple active managers	• highly structured • diversified in different asset classes • transparent, and easy to understand
Investors beliefs, behaviours, and actions	• assumes markets do not work • lacks an investment policy statement (IPS) • lacks an investment philosophy • unaware of behavioural biases • chases manager or fund performance • trades heavily • buys IPOs • attempts to time the market • bets on predictions	• steers clear of the eight common investment pitfalls • recognizes conflicts of interest in the financial services industry • avoids stock picking and market timing • regularly rebalances portfolio to maintain diversity • chooses passively-managed, index- or factor-based asset class investments • understands that risk and return are related and uses the Fama/French Three-Factor Model when constructing a portfolio • has a comprehensive IPS and investment philosophy • coordinates financial investments with life plan
Investor outcomes	• lack of transparency leads to confusion, less confidence in returns, and high stress and anxiety • poor performance or inconsistent returns • high fees and trading costs • negative tax consequences • vulnerable to manager drift and surprises • makes it more difficult to achieve personal goals	• clarity and transparency reduces stress and anxiety • higher and more consistent returns over the long term • lower fees and trading costs • tax consequences are minimized • better able to weather market fluctuations • immune to manager drift • increases the odds that personal goals are achieved

proven track record offer you the confidence and comfort of knowing that your investments are working for your interests, leaving you free to dedicate your energies and passions to the things that matter most: your family and friends, your business, and your retirement. By reading this book, you've taken the first step towards becoming an *empowered investor*. The blue ocean awaits.

APPENDIX

History of Portfolio Theory and Investment Management Breakthroughs

Prior to the 1920s: Investing in Stocks Limited to the Very Wealthy

Prior to the 1920s, only the truly wealthy in the United States and Canada had access to services enabling them to buy shares of publicly traded companies.

1924: Massachusetts Investors Trust, the World's First Mutual Fund, is created in Boston

The first official mutual fund in North America—the Massachusetts Investors Trust—was born on 21 March 1924. The mutual fund structure began the democratization process that gave investors real access to capital markets, allowing everyone to buy into equity markets in a diversified fashion.

Circa 1950: Conventional Wisdom

Although a few mutual funds did exist, mainstream investment thinking at this time was as follows: analyze securities one by one; focus on picking winners; and concentrate holdings to maximize returns. Broad diversification was considered undesirable. According to Gerald Loeb: "Once you attain competency, diversification is undesirable. One or two, or at most, three or four securities should be bought. Competent investors will never be satisfied beating the averages by a few small percentage points." (Gerald M. Loeb, *The Battle for Investment Survival*, 1935)

1952: Diversification and Portfolio Risk
Harry Markowitz, Nobel Prize in Economics, 1990

Markowitz conducted landmark research, concluding that diversification reduces risk, and redefined the concept of portfolio risk vs. security risk. Investors could construct an optimal portfolio to maximize return for a given standard deviation.

1958: The Role of Stocks
James Tobin, Nobel Prize in Economics, 1981

Tobin created the separation theorem, which has two tenets: form a portfolio of risky assets and temper the risk by lending and borrowing. Research shifted focus from stock selection to portfolio structure. ("Liquidity Preference as Behavior Toward Risk," *The Review of Economic Studies*, February 1958)

1961: Investments and Capital Structure
Merton Miller and Franco Modigliani, Nobel Prizes in Economics, 1985 and 1990

This research focused on determining the link between a company's corporate finance decisions and its company stock return and concluded that a firm's value is unrelated to its dividend policy. Dividend policy is therefore an unreliable guide for stock selection.

1964: Single-Factor Asset Pricing, Risk/Return Model
William Sharpe, Nobel Prize in Economics, 1990

Sharpe introduced the capital asset pricing model (CAPM), a theoretical model that defines risk as volatility relative to market. CAPM is used for evaluating the risk and expected return of securities and portfolios. A stock's cost of capital (the investor's expected return) is proportional to the stock's risk relative to the entire stock universe.

1965: Behaviour of Securities Price
Paul Samuelson, MIT, Nobel Prize in Economics, 1970

Samuelson came to several conclusions: market prices are the best estimates of value; price changes follow random patterns; and future stock prices are unpredictable. ("Proof That Properly Anticipated Prices Fluctuate Randomly," *Industrial Management Review*, Spring 1965)

1966: Efficient Markets Hypothesis
Eugene F. Fama, University of Chicago

Fama conducted extensive research on stock price trading patterns. He extended work on the unpredictability of stock prices and found that prices quickly incorporate information. Fama developed the "Efficient Markets Hypothesis" which asserts that prices reflect values and information accurately and quickly. It is difficult, if not impossible, to capture returns in excess of market returns without taking greater-than-market levels of risk. Investors cannot identify superior stocks using fundamental information or price patterns.

1968: First Major Studies of Manager Performance
Michael Jensen, 1965 and A.G. Becker Corporation, 1968

The first studies of U.S. mutual funds (Jensen) and institutional plans (A.G. Becker Corporation) indicated that active managers underperform the indexes. Becker Corp. started the financial consulting industry with the creation of "Green Book" performance tables comparing results to benchmarks. These were the first studies showing that investment professionals failed to outperform market indexes. (Michael Jensen, "The Performance of Mutual Funds in the Period 1945–1964," *Journal of Finance*, December 1965)

1972: Options Pricing Model
Fisher Black and Myron Scholes from the University of Chicago and Robert Merton of Harvard University, Nobel Prize in Economics, 1997

The development of the Options Pricing Model provided new ways to segment, quantify, and manage risk. It spurred the development of a market for alternative investments.

1973: Random Prices and Practical Investing
John McQuown, Wells Fargo Bank, 1971
Rex Sinquefield, American National Bank, 1973

We saw the birth of index funds as the banks developed the first passive S&P 500 Index funds.

1975: A Major Plan First Commits to Indexing
New York Telephone Company invests $40 million in an S&P 500 index fund.

The New York Telephone Company was the first major plan to index large U.S. companies. This helped launch the era of indexed investing. "Fund spokesmen are quick to point out you can't buy the market averages. It's time the public could." (Burton G. Malkiel, *A Random Walk Down Wall Street*, 1973)

1977: Database of Securities Prices Collects Extensive Public Market Information Dating Back to 1926
Roger Ibbotson and Rex Sinquefield
"Stocks, Bonds, Bills, and Inflation"

Researchers develop an extensive returns database for multiple asset classes. This new empirical database for evaluating asset class returns and assisting asset allocation decisions became one of the most widely used investment databases among institutional investors and changed the way institutional investors build portfolios.

1981: The Small Company Effect
Rolf Banz, University of Chicago

Banz researched NYSE stock returns from 1926–1975 and found that, in the long term, small companies have higher expected returns than large companies and behave differently.

1990: Nobel Prize Recognizes Modern Finance

Nobel recognized economists who have shaped the way we invest, emphasizing the role of science in finance. William Sharpe won for the Capital Asset Pricing Model, "beta," and relative risk. Harry Markowitz won for his work on portfolio diversification and the concept of risk and return.

1991: Determinants of Portfolio Performance
Brinson, Singer, and Beebower, Financial Analysts Journal, May 1991

This research assessed the impact of passive (benchmark) and active asset allocations and security selection on 82 large pension plans over the 1977–1987 period and discovered that, on average, benchmark asset allocation (allocation policy) explained 91.5% of the variation in quarterly returns.

1992: Multi-Factor Asset Pricing Model and Value Effect
Eugene Fama and Kenneth French, University of Chicago, Dartmouth College

Fama and French's research improved on the single-factor asset pricing model (CAPM). They published a landmark study, "The Cross Section of Expected Stock Returns," in the *Journal of Finance* (June 1992) and identified market, size, and value factors in returns. Their development of the three-factor asset pricing model is an invaluable asset allocation and portfolio analysis tool, and revolutionized the way investors and advisors construct and analyze portfolios.

2012: The Profitability Factor
Robert Novy-Marx

University of Rochester professor Robert Novy-Marx published "The Other Side of Value: The Gross Profitability Premium," asserting that a company's gross profitability has roughly the same weighting, and is complementary to, that company's book-to-market value when it comes to predicting its expected returns. His research concludes that profitable firms generate significantly higher returns than unprofitable firms (sorted by gross profits/assets).

2013: Nobel Prize Recognizes Research in the Empirical Analysis of Asset Prices

The Nobel Foundation recognized three economists who have laid the foundation for the current understanding of asset prices. Eugene F. Fama, Lars Peter Hansen and Robert J. Shiller shared the prize in economic sciences. Eugene Fama won for his work in developing the "Efficient Markets Hypothesis." His research laid the groundwork responsible for the development and growth of index funds all over the world.

1989 to Present: Evolution of Asset Class & Factor-Based Investment Tools

Canadian investors and investment advisors gained access to a broad selection of passively-managed asset class and factor based investment tools, empowering themselves to build better portfolios. Leading-edge portfolio construction concepts and strategies once reserved for large institutional investors can be implemented on a cost-effective basis for all investors.

Source: Dimensional Fund Advisors

NOTES

CHAPTER 1

1 Justin Kruger and David Dunning, "Unskilled and Unaware of It: How Difficulties in Recognizing One's Own Incompetence Lead to Inflated Self-Assessments," *Journal of Personality and Social Psychology* 77, no. 6 (1999): 1121–34.

2 Philip E. Tetlock, "Theory-Driven Reasoning about Plausible Pasts and Probable Futures in World Politics," *Heuristics and Biases: The Psychology of Intuitive Judgment*, edited by Gilovich, Griffin, and Kahneman, Cambridge University Press, 2002.

CHAPTER 2

1 "Regulatory Strategies for the Mid-90s: Recommendations for Regulating Investment Funds in Canada," the 1995 Stromberg Report. "Investment Funds in Canada and Consumer Protection: Strategies for the Millennium," the 1998 Stromberg Report.

2 Richard Sloan and two of his former doctoral students, Mark Bradshaw of Harvard Business School and Scott Richardson of the Wharton School at the University of Pennsylvania, examined data from more than 100,000 financial statements and stock returns for the years 1975 through 2000. They found that the degree of optimism in the earning forecasts, stock recommendations, and target prices of brokerage analysts is systematically related to corporate financing activities, especially for firms issuing new securities. "The economic significance of our results is striking," Sloan said. "For example, we find that target prices set by analysts are, on average, 80 percent too high for firms issuing securities versus only 20 percent too high for firms repurchasing securities."

CHAPTER 3

1 Dimensional study (2002) of 44 institutional equity pension plans with $452 billion total assets. Factor analysis run over various time periods, averaging 9 years. Total assets based on total plan dollar amounts as of December 2001. Average explanatory power (R2) is for the Fama/French equity benchmark universe.

2 Harry Markowitz's landmark research on portfolio theory was first published in 1952 in an essay entitled "Portfolio Selection." He later authored a book called *Portfolio Selection: Efficient Diversification* (1959). Markowitz's work on portfolio theory may be regarded as the foundation for applications of economic analysis in portfolio management.

CHAPTER 4

1 Sources for asset classes: Portfolio 1, S&P/TSX Composite Index; Portfolio 2, MSCI EAFE Index (net div.) = 33.3%, S&P 500 Index = 33.3%, S&P/TSX Composite Index = 33.4%; Portfolio 3, MSCI EAFE Index (net div.) = 30%, S&P 500 Index = 30%, S&P/TSX Composite Index = 30%, Dow Jones U.S. Select REIT Index = 10%; Portfolio 4, MSCI EAFE Value Index (net div.) = 10%, S&P 500 Index = 10%, S&P/TSX Composite Index = 30%, Dimensional International Small Cap Index = 10%, MSCI EAFE Index (net div.) = 10%, DFA U.S. Micro Cap Portfolio Class I = 10%, Dow Jones U.S. Select REIT Index = 10%, Russell 1000 Value Index = 10%.

CHAPTER 6

1 Studies support low-turnover index strategies. In a 1993 U.S. study on managing taxable portfolios, Robert H. Jeffrey and Robert D. Arnott concluded that taxes have a huge negative impact on relative returns and found that lower-turnover (stock-trading) index strategies were a more tax-efficient investment option than actively-traded mutual fund or investment counsellor strategies.

This report began the debate on tax-efficient investing within the investment management community in the United States. Prior to this report, no one cared or paid attention to tax-managed portfolios. This study remains highly regarded and is one of the outstanding contributions to the study of tax-efficient investing.

In 1996, Mike Thornfinnson and Jason Kiss published the first Canadian study on tax-efficient portfolio management, coming to essentially the same conclusions as the original U.S. study: over the long term, it is difficult to beat index strategies for taxable accounts.

These studies showed that, all pre-tax returns being equal, investors who use tax-efficient strategies will have more money in their taxable trading accounts after all the taxes are paid than investors who use traditional high-turnover mutual funds or trading-oriented investment counsellor offerings.

In fact, both studies concluded that actively-managed pools of capital (with lots of internal trading) would need to consistently outperform their benchmarks (after all their fees) by 100 to 200 basis points just to equal the after-tax returns of the lower-turnover index benchmarks.

CHAPTER 7

1 2013 Vanguard white paper entitled "Vanguard's Principles for Investing Success." Vanguard calculated the median manager performances versus benchmarks. First they assigned each fund to a representative benchmark according to both size and style (growth versus value). They then compared the performance of each fund to the performance of its style benchmark for each 36-month period since June 1992. Morningstar funds were grouped according to their star ratings and then Vanguard computed the median relative return versus the style benchmark for the subsequent 36-month period. Data are through December 2012. Data on cash flows, fund returns, and ratings were provided by Morningstar. Index data to compute relative excess returns were provided by Thomson Reuters Datastream. More information is available in the Vanguard research paper "Mutual Fund Ratings and Future Performance" (Philips and Kinniry 2010).

CHAPTER 8

1 Past performance is not a guarantee of future results. Values change frequently and past performance may not be repeated. There is always the risk that an investor may lose money. Securities of small firms are often less liquid than those of large companies. As a result, small company stocks may fluctuate relatively more in price. Even a long-term investment approach cannot guarantee a profit. Economic, political, and issuer-specific events will cause the value of securities, and the funds that own them, to rise or fall. Because the value of investments will fluctuate, there is a risk that investors will lose money.

2 Selection of funds, indices, and time periods presented chosen by client's advisor. Indices are not available for direct investment and performance does not reflect expenses of an actual portfolio. Past performance is not a guarantee of future results. Graph represents a hypothetical investment of $1. Performance includes reinvestment of dividends and capital gains. S&P 500 Index, MSCI EAFE Index (net div.), Dimensional Canada Small Value Index, Dimensional EAFE Small Value Index, Dimensional Emerging Markets Small Index, Dimensional Emer-

ging Markets Large Index, Dimensional U.S. Small Cap Value Index, S&P/TSX Composite Index.

CHAPTER 9

1 Marlena I. Lee, "From Premium to Dimension: Raising the Bar on Research," Dimensional Fund Advisors, June 2013, page 2.
2 Annualized compound returns of Canadian stocks in Canadian dollars. Annualized compound returns of U.S., International, and Emerging Market stocks in U.S. dollars. Methodology used for computing profitability premiums: Dimensional controls for relative price (BtM) and size (market cap) when computing the annualized compound returns for high and low profitability stocks in U.S. and non-U.S. developed markets, and controls only for size in emerging markets.

CHAPTER TEN

1 Andrew Ang and Knut N, Kjaer, "Investing for the Long Run," 11 November 2011. Available at SSRN: http://ssrn.com/abstract=1958258.

GLOSSARY

asset: Any resource capable of being owned and producing value.

asset allocation: An investment strategy whereby a portfolio is diversified across different asset classes to minimize risk.

asset class: A group of securities that display the same characteristics and behave similarly in the market and conform to the same rules and regulations. The three main asset classes are equities, fixed-income, and cash equivalents.

asset class fund: A diversified investment that tracks an index representing an asset class or alternatively a passively managed investment that provides an investor with direct exposure to a specific asset class.

Bay Street: The name of a street located in downtown Toronto where the headquarters of many Canadian banks and financial services companies are located. It has become a term used to refer to the centre of activity for financial services firms in Canada.

behavioural finance: The use of psychology-based theories to help explain stock market anomalies and why investors make certain decisions.

benchmark: A standard against which active money management can be measured or judged. Benchmarks exist for virtually every investable asset class and can be used by investors as a point of reference and comparison.

black swan: A random and unexpected event that could never have been foreseen. In relation to financial matters, could be an event that has a dramatic impact on investments (9/11, the rise of Google, or the collapse of Lehman Brothers are good examples of a black swan event).

bond: A debt security, whereby the issuer owes the investor a debt to be paid back with interest at certain dates. Federal, provincial, state, and/or municipal governments, along with major corporations, issue bonds to finance their budgets and operations. Institutional and individual investors typically invest in bonds as part of a diversified portfolio.

broad-based equity market: Typically refers to a well-diversified group (or index) of stocks that reflects the actions of an entire country market.

brokerage firm: A business that acts as an intermediary between buyers and sellers of securities and receives a commission from each successful transaction.

buy-and-hold: The investment strategy of buying certain securities with the intention of retaining them in a portfolio for the long term.

capital gain/loss: Capital gains are made when an investor sells a security at a greater price than it was purchased. Capital losses occur when an investor sells a security at a lesser price than it was purchased.

capital market: A market where both individuals and institutions trade securities.

Client Relationship Model (CRM): A 2012 initiative by the Canadian Security Administrators to enhance the level of care and disclosure of relationships between clients and investment professionals.

commission: A one-time service charge collected by a broker or advisor in return for providing advice or executing a transaction.

conflict of interest: A situation in which an advisor has a personal interest that makes him or her incapable of offering unbiased advice.

correlation (asset classes): The relationship between two asset classes during a given period of time. The concept of correlation is frequently used in portfolio analysis where benefits accrue to investors who hold non-correlated asset classes together.

cost of capital: The cost paid by the company to finance itself. It is also the required rate of return expected by investors for investing their money in a company or project.

diversification: The act or process of increasing the number of asset classes (within a portfolio) or the number of securities (within an asset class). This strategy is used to help investors manage investment risk.

deferred service charge (DSC): This may also be referred to as a "deferred" or "back-end" sales load. This charge is levied when an investor cashes in a mutual fund with this particular type of mechanism. The charge can be up to 5 or 6% of the value of the investment being redeemed, but varies inversely with the time period the mutual fund has been owned. In general, an investor who has owned a fund for more than seven years is not subject to the DSC charges.

exchange traded fund (ETF): A mutual fund that trades like a stock on a stock exchange. ETFs are made up of diversified holdings that typically track an index or commercial benchmark. ETFs are considered index investments and have high levels of transparency and very low fees.

Fama/French Three-Factor Model: The Fama/French Three-Factor Model is a multi-factor asset pricing model designed in 1992 by Eugene Fama and Kenneth French to describe stock returns.

fee-based management: An advisory approach whereby the advisory firm (or advisor) is paid an annual retainer for ongoing advice and access to unbiased solutions. Fees are typically 1.00% of assets under management but can vary depending on the size of the portfolio.

fixed income product: An investment (such as a bond) that pays interest (income) on a regular basis to its investors.

growth stock: A stock in a company whose earnings are expected to increase at a higher rate relative to the market. Growth companies tend to have higher valuation levels (such as P/E ratios) than value companies.

home bias: The tendency to overwhelmingly invest in domestic equities in the belief that they are a better investment than foreign equities. This bias occurs in many countries at the individual investor level as most investors seem to have a preference for investing in local companies. Reducing home bias in investor portfolios improves diversification.

index investing: An investment approach that allocates investment dollars to one or a variety of investments that will track and try to replicate the rate of return of an underlying market index. Investors use vehicles such as ETFs or index funds to track the performance of a specific index.

investment philosophy: A set of guiding principles that shape and inform the investment decision-making process of an individual, an advisor, or an advisory firm; a code of conduct defining how investment funds will be managed.

Initial Public Offering (IPO): A private company's first sale of stock to the public.

Investment Policy Statement (IPS): A written document outlining an investment strategy and goals. The IPS brings clarity, vision, and discipline to the investment process and keeps investors on track.

loss aversion: The tendency of people to strongly prefer avoiding losses over attaining gains. Studies suggest that, psychologically, losses are as much as twice as powerful as gains.

market capitalization: The total market value of the outstanding shares of a company.

market forecasting: The act of trying to predict future market movements.

market timing: The act of attempting to make profits (or protect gains) in a stock portfolio by transferring investment dollars between asset classes in anticipation of a forecasted market event.

management expense ratio (MER): An investment company's cost of operating a fund. It is determined by dividing the value of the fund's expenses by the value of the fund's assets under management.

MSCI EAFE Index: An index measuring the performance of combined capitalization weighted equity markets in Europe, Australasia, and the Far East.

mutual fund: An investment vehicle composed of a pool of funds collected by different investors for the purpose of investing in market securities. The gains and losses are shared proportionately among the investors.

opportunity cost: The difference in return between the investment that was made and the best alternative that was passed up.

passive investing: Following an investment strategy in which a fund manager invests in a pre-determined strategy that does not entail any forecasting of market or stock directions. Typically the fund will track either an index or try to capture the returns of an asset class or set of style and/or capitalization factors through a rule-based investment approach.

price/earnings ratio (P/E): The ratio of a company's stock price to its earnings.

pension fund: A common employee fund sponsored by an employer to facilitate the investment of the employees' retirement funds. The fund's investment mandates are long-term in nature.

performance chasing: Allocating investment dollars to areas or investments that have just recently gone up in value or have performed extremely well relative to other portfolio options. Often investors look at past returns and invest in the highest return investments (whether that be hot asset class or high manager returns) only to find out that they caught the upper end of the wave. The investments underperform and the investment experience is not a positive one relative to that of other comparable investments. It is a very dangerous investment habit to follow.

Ponzi scheme: An investment scam that promises high returns with low risks to investors and is usually done in a non-regulated environment. The person running the scheme pays his early investors with the money given to him by new investors. The scam can continue as long as there are more new investors.

portfolio: A grouping of financial assets held directly by investors. A portfolio is usually composed of stocks, bonds, cash equivalents, etc.

portfolio theory: A theory pioneered by Harry Markowitz in the 1950s that aims to maximize expected returns based on a given level of market risk.

premium (investment): An excess return of one form of investment relative to another form.

premium (equity): The excess return of an individual stock or of the overall market itself over a risk-free rate. This premium compensates investors for investing in higher-risk investments relative to the risk-free rate. There is no guarantee that the equity premium will exist over the short term; investors seeking to capture this premium must stay committed to their long-term allocations.

premium (value): The excess return of high book-to-market stocks (value stocks) over low book-to-market stocks (growth stocks). This premium compensates investors for investing in higher-risk value companies relative to growth companies. There is no guarantee that the value premium will exist over the short term and investors seeking to capture this premium must stay committed to their long-term allocations.

premium (size): The excess return of small company stocks over large company stocks. This premium compensates investors for investing in higher-risk small companies relative to large companies. There is no guarantee that the small company premium will exist over the short term; investors seeking to capture this premium must stay committed to their long-term allocations.

premium (profitability): The excess return of high gross profitability company stocks over low gross profitability company stocks. Identified and quantified in June 2012 by Robert Novy-Marx in "The Other Side of Value: The Gross Profitability Premium." More work remains to be done to discover how best to include this premium on a passive basis in the design of portfolios.

public equity: A stock or security that can be bought or sold on a stock exchange representing an ownership position of a publicly-traded company.

rebalancing: The process of buying or selling asset class positions within a portfolio to address imbalances in portfolio positions that have occurred due to different asset class price trends. This is done by realigning the current asset allocation back to the long-term target.

recession: A decline in economic activity with visible effects in industrial production, employment, real income, and trade. A recession exists after two consecutive quarters of negative GDP growth.

Registered Retirement Savings Plan (RRSP): A legal trust that is registered with the Canada Revenue Agency that helps Canadians save for retirement by allowing them to make tax-deductible contributions to their plans. The growth of investments within an RRSP is tax sheltered. Investments within an RRSP can be in the form of stocks, bonds, mutual funds, etc. Withdrawals from the RRSP during retirement are taxed at the marginal tax rate of the holder at that time.

S&P 500 Index: An index made up of the leading 500 companies on the New York Stock Exchange.

S&P/TSX Composite Index: An index made up of the largest companies on the Toronto Stock Exchange.

safe retirement draw-down rate: The percentage of a portfolio that can be withdrawn during retirement without running out of funds.

Single-Factor Pricing Model (also known as the Capital Asset Pricing Model [CAPM]): A financial model that describes the relationship between risk and expected return for a security. Later supplanted by multi-factor financial models such as the Fama/French Three-Factor Model.

small company stock: In the United States, a company with a market capitalization between $300 million and $2 billion. Canadian small companies will have smaller capitalization sizes.

stock picking: Within the context of asset class investing, choosing individual securities within an asset class in an attempt to outperform the asset class benchmarks.

survivorship bias: The result of not including mutual funds that performed poorly and were subsequently closed or consolidated in calculations of the average of mutual fund median manager performance. Including the results of the "winners" or successful funds and excluding the results of the "losers" or poorly-performing funds skews the average results upwards. Survivorship bias makes the group as a whole appear to have better performance than what was actually achieved within the starting group.

sustainability (financial): Financial sustainability is achieved when individuals are able to build sufficient financial assets during their working years to sustain a comfortable retirement, however long or short it may be. This typically means building a lifestyle during one's working years where one lives within one's means. Annual and regular savings are key components of building a sustainable lifestyle.

time horizon: The duration an investment is held before it is sold. The time horizon depends on the investment goals of each individual investor and the risks that investor is willing to take.

transparency (relationship): The level of disclosure and clarity concerning the relationship between advisory firms (or advisors) and their clients on items such as how they will operate and work together, the price and cost of services rendered, reporting standards, and disclosing potential conflicts, etc.

transparency (investment): The level of disclosure and clarity between advisory firms (or advisors) and their clients with respect to investments, including such items as investment philosophy and code of conduct, reporting on current-vs.-target asset allocation, factor loading (small company, value company etc.), and diversification characteristics of a portfolio.

unbiased advice: In the context of financial advice, advice that is fair and impartial and has no bias or prejudice. Recommendations are not influenced by advisor conflicts of interest and are for the sole benefit of the client.

underwriting: The process used by investment banks to raise investment capital from investors for governments or corporations that are issuing securities.

unemployment rate: The percentage of the workforce that is currently unemployed but actively seeking work.

value investing: An investment style based on ideas that Ben Graham and David Dodd began teaching at Columbia Business School in 1928. Generally involves investing in securities that appear underpriced by some form of fundamental analysis (i.e. companies that trade at discounts to book value, have high dividend yields, have low price-to-earnings multiples, or have low price-to-book ratios). Numerous academics have demonstrated that, over the long run, value stocks consistently outperform growth stocks and the market as a whole.

volatility: A measure of the difference in returns for any given security or index.

Wall Street: The Manhattan street where the New York Stock Exchange is located. Many of the headquarters of U.S. banks and financial services companies can be found in the same area. Has become the term used to refer to the centre of activity for financial services firms in the U.S.

ACKNOWLEDGMENTS

It is a great pleasure to thank the many people who have made this book and its third edition possible. This is the most comprehensive and in-depth edition of *The Empowered Investor* to date. It has everything that I think is important for all Canadian investors to know.

When I set out to write the first edition nine years ago, I never suspected that I would be writing a third edition in 2013. Why did I choose to publish subsequent editions? I believe that the timeless principles of *The Empowered Investor* have the power to change and improve investors' lives and their investment experiences. This investment philosophy merits repeating and the use of the most up-to-date evidence and data in order to show investors that its benefits apply in all market conditions. By reminding investors why this investment philosophy works, I hope to inspire them to follow through with it and take action. Today's frenzied and hype-driven world offers a multitude of distractions that can lead investors down the wrong path. By advocating for conflict-free investment advice, I believe I can help investors see clear solutions in an otherwise murky world. I look forward to writing new editions in the future as events require.

Since the day I left my job as a bond trader to become a private client advisor in 1995, I have been pursuing these investment concepts and principles with clients, family, and friends. I have seen these principles work with all types of investors in all types of market conditions. I owe special thanks to my clients, for together we have embraced and stayed committed to these principles in our quest to become empowered investors. They have always been respectful and asked great questions, which has pushed me to learn more and to strive to communicate these ideas as best I can. I am so grateful for the opportunity to work with them.

A special thank you to all my former and current professional colleagues: our collective efforts and collaboration have encouraged me to develop a strong sense of independent investment thinking. In today's world of Canadian bank dominance and tied selling strategies, it takes conviction for independents to stand up and tell their stories. I would have it no other way. From Casgrain & Company, to PWL Capital and to my present firm, Tulett, Matthews & Associates, and a best practice network called Final Frontier of which I am a member, I owe so much gratitude to so many wonderful and dedicated professionals. In addition, I have had the pleasure of meeting many great Canadian and U.S. advisors who share in this investment approach. From the few dozen or so Canadian advisors I knew doing business this way in the mid-1990s to the few hundred practicing today, I have made many friends and we have shared many learning experiences together. Each of you is part of this story.

This book would not have been possible without the incredible openness of the academic investment community across North America. Over the years, I have had the privilege of meeting many researchers from both Canada and the United States, and their work has been truly inspirational. Through published research reports, investment conferences, web sites, telephone conversations, and more, they have taught me some very important concepts about investing.

And finally, much credit is owed to the editorial and creative team of this book. Connor McRae was my right-hand man throughout this third edition. He was responsible for editing, researching and adding tone and additional commentary to many sections. From the array of professional options open to him, Connor has chosen to pursue his passion—writing. At the age of twenty-two, he has already written two books. He is an inspiring and wise young man and I wish him all the best as he pursues his love of writing and his dreams. Garet Markvoort and David Drummond did an outstanding job in bringing the book to life with their wonderful interior layout and book jacket design, respectively. They brought a fresh look and feel to a personal finance book that is so fitting for *The Empowered Investor.*

It truly was a team effort.

Thank you all.
Keith Matthews

ABOUT THE AUTHOR

For nearly 20 years, Keith Matthews has been a steadfast proponent of the winning investment principles and benefits of passive investing found in this book. Through his client advisory business, Keith has helped his clients build better wealth management strategies to reach their long-term goals. This third edition of The Empowered Investor is a Canadian guide to the philosophy and principles he has championed throughout his career.

In 1993, while working as an institutional bond trader, Keith purchased his first ETF in his personal RRSP account. He purchased TIPS (Toronto 35 Index Participation units) in his retirement account and from this point on he pursued his interest and research in asset class investment strategies.

As a partner and portfolio manager at Tulett, Matthews & Associates, Keith continues to work closely with clients using the same investment principles described in this book: long-term asset allocation, diversification, discipline, using passively-managed asset class investments, and tilting portfolios to value and small cap factors, among others.

Keith's articles and views concerning asset allocation strategies, portfolio management tools, and trends in the financial services industry have frequently appeared in a variety of Canadian media sources, and he has shared his views at various industry conferences. He holds an MBA from the Richard Ivey School of Business at the University of Western Ontario and is a Chartered Investment Manager.

Married and the father of three energetic children, Keith Matthews lives in Beaconsfield, Quebec, and enjoys squash, skiing, sailing, and rugby—perhaps a little less rugby and a little more sailing as the years progress!

Contact Information:
Keith Matthews
Partner and Portfolio Manager
keith@tma-invest.com
www.tma-invest.com

For more information about this book, please visit
www.empoweredinvestor.ca